1 MONTH OF FREE READING

at

www.ForgottenBooks.com

By purchasing this book you are eligible for one month membership to ForgottenBooks.com, giving you unlimited access to our entire collection of over 1,000,000 titles via our web site and mobile apps.

To claim your free month visit:

www.forgottenbooks.com/free854866

ISBN 978-0-483-30469-7
PIBN 10854866

..iche
s
ographs)

Collection de
microfiches
(monographies)

Histoıical Microredroductions/Institut canadien de micıoıepıoductions historiq

2000

Technical and Bibliographic Notes / Notes techni

The Institute has attempted to obtain the best original copy available for filming. Features of this copy which may be bibliographically unique, which may alter any of the images in the reproduction, or which may significantly change the usual method of filming are checked below.

L'Institut a m
été possible d
plaire qui son
ographique, q
ou qui peuve
de normale de

- [✓] Coloured covers /
  Couverture de couleur

- [ ] Covers damaged /
  Couverture endommagée

- [ ] Covers restored and/or laminated /
  Couverture restaurée et/ou pelliculée

- [ ] Cover title missing / Le titre de couverture manque

- [ ] Coloured maps / Cartes géographiques en couleur

- [ ] Coloured ink (i.e. other than blue or black) /
  Encre de couleur (i.e. autre que bleue ou noire)

- [✓] Coloured plates and/or illustrations /
  Planches et/ou illustrations en couleur

- [ ] Bound with other material /
  Relié avec d'autres documents

- [ ] Only edition available /
  Seule édition disponible

- [ ] Tight binding may cause shadows or distortion along interior margin / La reliure serrée peut causer de l'ombre ou de la distorsion le long de la marge intérieure.

- [ ] Blank leaves added during restorations may appear within the text. Whenever possible, these have been omitted from filming / Il se peut que certaines pages blanches ajoutées lors d'une restauration apparaissent dans le texte, mais, lorsque cela était possible, ces pages n'ont pas été filmées.

- [ ] Additional comments /
  Commentaires supplémentaires:

- [ ] Coloure

- [ ] Pages d

- [ ] Pages r
  Pages r

- [✓] Pages d
  Pages d

- [ ] Pages d

- [✓] Showthr

- [ ] Quality c
  Qualité i

- [ ] Includes
  Compre

- [ ] Pages w
  tissues,
  possibl
  partielle
  pelure,
  obtenir l

- [ ] Opposi
  discolou
  possible
  coloratic
  filmées
  possible.

best quality
nd legibility of
h the filming

Les images suivantes ont été reproduites avec le
plus grand soin, compte tenu de la condition et de
la netteté de l'exemplaire filmé, et en conformité
avec les conditions du contrat de filmage.

ers are filmed
ending on the
d impression, or
All other original
first page with a
d ending on the
d impression.

Les exemplaires originaux dont la couverture en
papier est imprimée sont filmés en commençant
par le premier plat et en terminant soit par la
dernière page qui comporte une empreinte d'impression ou d'illustration, soit par le second plat,
selon le cas. Tous les autres exemplaires originaux sont filmés en commençant par la première
page qui comporte une empreinte d'impression ou
d'illustration et en terminant par la dernière page
qui comporte une telle empreinte.

icrofiche shall
NTINUED"), or
ichever applies.

Un des symboles suivants apparaîtra sur la
dernière image de chaque microfiche, selon le cas:
le symbole → signifie "A SUIVRE", le symbole ▼
signifie "FIN".

ilmed at
o large to be
re filmed begin-
eft to right and
equired. The
thod:

Les cartes, planches, tableaux, etc., peuvent être
filmés à des taux de réduction différents. Lorsque
le document est trop grand pour être reproduit en
un seul cliché, il est filmé à partir de l'angle
supérieur gauche, de gauche à droite, et de haut
en bas, en prenant le nombre d'images
nécessaire. Les diagrammes suivants illustrent la
méthode.

3

1

MICROCOPY RESOLUTION TEST CHART

ANSI and ISO TEST CHART No 2

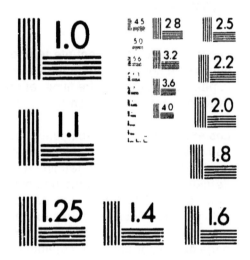

APPLIED IMAGE Inc

1653 East Main Street
Rochester, New York 14609 USA
Phone
5989 – Fax

FOUNDERS OF THE EMPIRE

ALFRED AT WORK IN HIS STUDY.

"OUR EMPIRE" SERIES

FOUNDERS OF THE EMPIRE

BY

PHILIP GIBBS

WITH FOUR COLOURED PLATES

AND NUMEROUS ILLUSTRATIONS

FIFTEENTH THOUSAND

First Edition *September* 1899
Reprinted 1901, 1903, 1907.

PREFACE.

THE object which this book is intended to serve is very simple, and may be explained in a few lines.

At the present day the number of books is infinite, and to the host of books should be added the great array of serials, weekly papers, daily papers, snippets, snaps and collections of extracts of all sorts and kinds which form the principal reading matter of the English-speaking peoples. It has been said that "in the multitude of counsellors there is wisdom." The statement comes to us on high authority, but its self-evident truth will not entirely commend itself to all minds. In the multitude of books, at any rate, there is often very little wisdom, and there are thousands of readers who, in their anxiety to know "something about everything," never come within measurable distance of knowing "everything about something." So superficial does the reading of many persons become that whole departments of knowledge—historical, literary, scientific—are represented in their minds only by a series of words and names which are used like counters or algebraical symbols to represent real values behind them. Unluckily, in playing the game, or doing the sum, the real values have in many cases dropped altogether out of sight and knowledge, and the players or calculators are quite unable to state their true nature and value. This state of things exists in relation to every branch of knowledge, but it is perhaps specially marked in the case of great books and great men. Out of ten thousand persons who talk about Homer and Virgil, not half a dozen are really familiar with the *Odyssey* or the *Æneid*. The expression "Milton" has become a counter representing a value which is admitted, but of which, as a rule, nothing whatever is known ; and the catalogue of instances might be indefinitely extended, so common is the practice of playing literary counters which the players can never redeem.

The same thing is true in the case of great men and women. We play "Shakespeare" as representing a great poet, but we do not all read Shakespeare. "Newton" stands for science in the speech and writing of many who have never heard of the "Principia" and have not the faintest idea as to the subjects of which it treats. "Machiavelli" represents craft in politics in the minds of those who do not know to within a thousand years when he lived, or to within a thousand miles where he lived. In the same way even such famous names as Hannibal, Cæsar, Charlemagne, Alfred, Voltaire, are names only to most of those who use them. That this ignorance should exist is, of course, inevitable. No man can have the whole biographical dictionary at his fingers' ends. But the want of knowledge exists to a far greater extent than it ought to do or need do, because modern readers have, to a great extent, given up any reference to originals, and have abandoned standard works for the delights of literary snippets and summaries.

It is when we come to the history of our own country that we find out how much is lost by this practice. It is of great importance that an Englishman should know something of the great men of his race—should understand what they did, why they did it, and to what extent Britain is indebted to them for what they suffered and what they achieved. It will be a misfortune if the day ever comes when the names of great Englishmen become counters merely. It is with the object of postponing this day—of enabling readers, young and old, to redeem the counters which have hitherto represented nothing of real value to them—that this book is written. In its pages are to be found brief and very simple biographies of some of the greatest Englishmen—men who in their day, each in his different manner, contributed to make Britain great, good, glorious, and free. All are not equally noble, all are not equally deserving of our admiration; but they have left behind them "footprints in the sands of time." They have all done something which we, their successors in bearing the burden of Empire, may admire, and which, in our degree, we may emulate and imitate.

CONTENTS.

PAGE

I.
ALFRED, THE MODEL OF ENGLISH KINGS 1

II.
STEPHEN LANGTON AND THE GREAT CHARTER . . . 12

III.
SIMON DE MONTFORT AND THE RISE OF THE ENGLISH
PARLIAMENT 59

IV.
SIR FRANCIS DRAKE AND THE NEW WORLD . . . 86

V.
JOHN HAMPDEN AND THE DEFENCE OF ENGLISH LIBERTY 127

VI.
ADMIRAL BLAKE AND THE SUPREMACY AT SEA . . . 146

VII.
LORD CLIVE AND THE INDIAN EMPIRE 163

VIII.
GENERAL WOLFE AND THE DOMINION OF CANADA . . 188

IX.
WILLIAM PITT, EARL OF CHATHAM, AND ENGLISH STATES-
MANSHIP 209

X.
CAPTAIN COOK AND THE EXPLORATION OF AUSTRALASIA . 226

XI.
NELSON AND WELLINGTON AND THE DEFENCE OF THE
EMPIRE 240

LIST OF ILLUSTRATIONS.

	PAGE
ALFRED AT WORK IN HIS STUDY (*Coloured Plate*) . . *Frontispiece*	
MAP OF ENGLAND, SHOWING THE ANGLO-SAXON KINGDOMS · ·	10
HOW THE DANES CAME UP THE CHANNEL A THOUSAND YEARS AGO.	12
ALFRED'S MOTHER READING ALOUD	15
THE WHITE HORSE BETWEEN DIDCOT AND SWINDON · · ·	28
ALFRED'S JEWEL	29
A VIKING CHIEF	39
A SEAL OF STEPHEN LANGTON	44
KING JOHN SIGNING MAGNA CHARTA·	53
THE QUARREL BETWEEN SIMON AND KING HENRY · . .	65
THE BARONS ASKING HENRY III. TO SUMMON A PARLIAMENT (*Coloured Plate*) *To face*	78
THE ARMS OF SIMON DE MONTFORT	85
SIR FRANCIS DRAKE	87
CITIZENS IN THE DAYS OF DRAKE · · · · ·	92
THE ARMADA COMING UP THE CHANNEL · · · · ·	117
A REMNANT OF THE "INVINCIBLE ARMADA" · · · ·	124
JOHN HAMPDEN	127
CHARLES I.	129
THE SPEAKER HELD DOWN IN HIS CHAIR · · · ·	133
THE ARREST OF STRAFFORD	137
WESTMINSTER HALL IN THE TIME OF CHARLES I. . . . '.	142
HAMPDEN MORTALLY WOUNDED AT CHALGROVE FIELD (*Coloured Plate*) *To face*	144
ADMIRAL BLAKE	147
PRINCE RUPERT	150
IN THE DOWNS	154
LORD CLIVE	164
CLIVE AT ARCOT	169
CLIVE RECEIVING MEER JAFFIER AT PLASSEY (*Coloured Plate*) *To face*	180
JAMES WOLFE	189
MAP OF THE SIEGE OF QUEBEC, 1759.	195
WILLIAM PITT, LORD CHATHAM	210
SIR ROBERT WALPOLE	217
CAPTAIN COOK	227
THE *ENDEAVOUR* APPROACHING TAHITI	231
NAPOLEON BUONAPARTE	241
NELSON COMING ON DECK BEFORE THE BATTLE OF TRAFALGAR .	247
NELSON'S DEATH IN THE COCKPIT OF THE *VICTORY*. . .	249
THE DUKE OF WELLINGTON	252
THE WELLINGTON MEMORIAL IN ST. PAUL'S CATHEDRAL . .	255

FOUNDERS OF THE EMPIRE.

I.

ALFRED.

THE MODEL OF ENGLISH KINGS.

"I do not know if there has ever been on earth a man more worthy of the admiration of posterity than Alfred the Great."--Voltaire.

ANYONE who reads the pages of English history will find many characters worthy of his admiration and reverence. He will read the story of great kings and queens, wise statesmen, brave warriors and honest citizens. The greatness of the British Empire has been built up by the wisdom, the courage, and the industry of these men and women, and every citizen of the Empire, worthy of the name, will always remember and be proud of them. But it is often disappointing to find that, in spite of the great qualities of these people, most of them also possessed the faults common to mankind. Many great kings and queens have been cruel or unjust, many great statesmen have been greedy for wealth or power, and brave warriors have often been proud and overbearing. The farther back one reads in English history the more is this apparent. In the early ages the world was like a rough and noisy schoolboy, fond of fighting, who has not yet learnt to restrain his passions and to love law and order.

There is one character, however, in the early years of English history which stands out like a bright star in the darkness of night. This is Alfred the Great, King of the Saxons.

In an age when men neglected learning, Alfred was eager to gain knowledge and wisdom, and to teach them to his people. When most men were rough and cruel, Alfred was gentle and merciful. When kings were often proud and tyrannous, Alfred was humble and just. When Christian countries had almost forgotten their religion in their struggles against a host of barbarians, Alfred always strove to lead a true Christian life and to teach his countrymen to do the same.

Fortunately we can learn more about his character than in the case of many English kings, for he had a friend and servant, named Asser, who wrote down the story of his master's life. This story is still to be read by anyone who wishes to learn about the wisest of English kings. Everyone can read how Alfred struggled for years against the enemies of England, until by his heroism he saved his country and gave it peace and prosperity. One can read how, in spite of a dreadful disease which gave him no comfort day or night, he devoted his life to the welfare of his people, and how, in spite of his difficulties in obtaining teachers, he became a learned scholar and wrote books for the education of his countrymen, which still interest and instruct scholars of our own day.

In the following pages we shall tell the story
of Alfred's life in fewer words than those of his
friend, Bishop Asser, but before doing so it will be
well to give a brief survey of the state of England
before Alfred came into the world.

THE BEGINNING OF "ENGLE-LAND."

In the year 449 a horde of sea-pirates landed on
the coast of Kent and attacked the Britons, who
defended their shores from the fierce invaders.
Shortly afterwards other fleets of pirates from the
same parts swept down upon the shores of Britain.
They were strong, fair-haired, blue-eyed men, and
they came across the sea from the country we now
call Germany. They belonged to three great tribes
or nations, called Angles, Saxons, and Jutes. Foot
by foot the Britons were beaten back, until, after
many years of fighting, the Angles and Saxons became masters of the whole of Britain except Wales,
Cornwall and Strathclyde, in which the descendants
of the early Britons still live.

When the Angles and Saxons had conquered the
country, they abandoned their sea-faring life and
devoted themselves to clearing the forests, tilling
the ground, and building towns. Gradually the
island came to be called England, or the land of
the Angles. For a long time, however, the country
was divided into a number of different kingdoms—
such as Sussex (the kingdom of the *South* Saxons),
Wessex (the kingdom of the *West* Saxons), Northumbria
(the kingdom *North of the Humber*), and so on.
These kingdoms were nearly always at war with one
another, and sometimes one became more powerful,

sometimes another. At last, when Egbert, the grandfather of Alfred, became King of Wessex (which consisted of Somersetshire, Dorset, Wiltshire,

MAP OF ENGLAND, SHOWING THE ANGLO-SAXON KINGDOMS.

Hampshire, Berkshire, and Devonshire), the other kings acknowledged his authority over them, and he became the first "Over-lord" or King of all England.

And now the descendants of the fair-haired pirates who had swept down upon the coast of

Britain and conquered the land by hard fighting, were in their turn attacked by swarms of sea-warriors who sailed from the North to kill and plunder.

These fresh bands of warriors who came to molest the English shores were called Northmen, or *Danes.* Some of them came from Denmark, from which country they obtained their name, but most of them sailed from the rugged coasts of Norway and Sweden. In those days Norway, Sweden and Denmark were ruled by a great number of petty kings. The eldest sons of these kings were, generally, the heirs to their fathers' land, but the younger sons had no property except their ships, and no power in their own country except the crews who manned their vessels, and the might of their swords.

These men were called Vikings. They swarmed upon the ocean, and attacked any shore to which the wind and waves might carry them. They gloried in fighting and bloodshed, and they strove to gain the admiration of their countrymen by the daring of their attacks on foreign nations, and their deeds of cruelty and destruction.

It is no wonder that the Saxons were filled with dread when they saw the long-ships of the North approach the coast of England. The wind filled their sails, on which were painted dragons, ravens, and other creatures; or, if the wind fell, they were rowed by thirty pairs of oars, while the Vikings chanted their war-songs and waved their heavy axes in defiance.

The Northmen first appeared off the coast of England in the year 787, and after that date they made frequent attacks. The English were in constant

HOW THE DANES CAME UP THE CHANNEL A THOUSAND YEARS AGO.

(*From the Picture by Herbert A. Bone.*)

alarm, and in their prayers which they offered up
in the churches they added the words—

"*From the fury of the Northmen, good Lord deliver us!*"

They called the Northmen "the Locusts of the Baltic,"
for in the same way that a swarm of locusts destroys
the harvests of the East, so the Northmen came
from the Baltic Sea and, with flame and sword,
turned lands full of prosperous villages and pleasant
meadows into uninhabited deserts.

It was at a time when England was in deadly
peril from the Northmen that Alfred, who was to
deliver his country from its enemies, was born at
Wantage, in Berkshire, in the year 849.

ALFRED'S CHILDHOOD.

Alfred was the son of Ethelwulph, King of Wessex.
His mother was Osberga, the daughter of the king's
cup-bearer. At first it did not seem likely that
Alfred would ever become king, for he had three
brothers older than himself, named Ethelbald, Ethel-
bert, and Ethelred. Each of these became King of
Wessex in turn, but their lives were short, and
when Ethelred, the youngest of them, died, the
throne was left vacant for Alfred, who was then only
twenty-one years old.

Bishop Asser tells us that Alfred "was loved by
his father and mother, and even by all the people,
above all his brothers, and was educated altogether
at the court of the king. As he advanced through
the years of infancy and youth, his form appeared
more comely than that of his brothers; in look,
in speech and in manners he was more graceful
than they."

When Alfred was five years old, his father sent him on a journey to Rome with a number of Saxon nobles. Although King Ethelwulph had three sons older than Alfred, he seems to have wished him to be his successor, for the little boy was anointed king by the Pope at Rome at the request of his father.

Alfred returned to England, but two years later his father, who was now an old man, set out for Rome himself, taking with him his youngest and favourite son. They travelled through France, and here Alfred made the acquaintance of a learned bishop named Grimbald, who, many years later, came over to England at Alfred's invitation, and became one of his greatest friends and most learned teachers.

For a whole year Alfred remained with his father at Rome. This city had formerly been the most splendid in the world. It was filled with magnificent palaces and temples, very different from the wooden houses or the rough stone castles of the Anglo-Saxons. They must have struck the mind of an intelligent boy like Alfred with admiration and awe.

On the way home again, the Saxon king and his son stayed for a while at the court of France. Even in those days Frenchmen (or *Franks*, as they were then called) were renowned for their politeness and for the cultivation of learning. Alfred no doubt remarked the contrast between their behaviour and the rough, uncouth manners of his own countrymen.

Perhaps it was at this time that he was first filled with that desire for knowledge which never departed from him during his life.

After his return to England Alfred led a quiet

life among the Saxon nobles and people of whom he was, one day, to be king.

From his earliest childhood he was passionately fond of listening to the Saxon poems which used to be recited at the king's court. We are told that, by day and night, whenever he could get an opportunity, he would listen to this poetry which described

ALFRED'S MOTHER READING ALOUD.

in rough verse the brave deeds of Saxon kings or chiefs, or stories of the saints and martyrs. In after days Alfred himself became a poet, but it was not until he was twelve years old that he learnt to read.

One day his mother was sitting in the midst of her family with a manuscript of Saxon poetry in her hands. The book was beautifully illuminated

—that is to say, illustrated with richly coloured initial letters and designs. A happy idea struck the queen, and she offered the book as a gift to the son who should be first able to read it. Alfred's brothers were much older than himself, and, perhaps, smiled at the idea of taking so much trouble for such a small reward. Alfred, however, who was a boy of twelve, cherished his mother's words in his heart and resolved to strive for the prize. He found out an instructor, and it was not long before he was able to tell his mother that he could read her book of Saxon poetry, and claimed it according to her promise.

In these days, as soon as a boy can read his native language, he has opened the door to a world of wonder and delight. The knowledge which wise men of every age have discovered is offered to him if he has the will and the sense to accept the gift. In Alfred's time it was different. There were very few books written in the Saxon language. Most of the works of the learned authors of Europe were written in Latin, and if a person did not know that language, it was impossible for him to obtain much book-knowledge. Before the Danes had destroyed the peace of England this was not of much consequence, because the priests, who at that time were the teachers, were all good Latin scholars, and any Saxon boy whose parents could afford to have him educated could very easily learn that language. When, however, the terrible " Locusts of the Baltic " swept down upon the coast of England, they destroyed the monasteries, killed a great number of priests, and burnt their books. For a long time

the Saxons had to think more about defending their
homes than about book-knowledge, and by degrees
there came to be very few people in England who
could understand Latin. Bishop Asser relates that
Alfred frequently complained with deep sorrow that
"when he had the age, permission, and ability to
learn, he could find no masters." As we shall see
later on, it was not until Alfred was thirty-nine
years old that he obtained the happiness of reading
the Latin authors in their original language.

"THE LOCUSTS OF THE BALTIC."

When Alfred's brother Ethelred succeeded to
the throne of Wessex, and Alfred himself was eighteen
years of age, the Anglo-Saxons were terrified by the
news of a huge fleet of Vikings who were preparing
to invade England. One of their greatest chiefs,
named Ragnar Lodbrog, who had earned the admiration of his countrymen by his terrible deeds throughout Europe, had been wrecked upon the coast of
Northumbria, the most northerly kingdom of England.
At last he found himself powerless in the hands of
his enemies, and Ella, the King of Northumbria,
condemned him to a cruel death.

When this news reached the kingdoms of the
Northmen, they swore to revenge themselves for
the death of the man whose deeds had been their
pride. Vikings from the bays and fiords of Norway,
Sweden, Denmark, Jutland, and Russia, assembled
to share in this revenge. This great fleet was commanded by eight kings and twenty earls, the
children and relatives of Ragnar Lodbrog.

In the year 867 they sailed out of the Baltic,

B

and shortly afterwards they reached the shores of
East Anglia, as the counties of Norfolk, Suffolk, and
Lincolnshire were then called. During the winter
they did not attack the Anglo-Saxons, but they
remained quietly in their camp, collecting provisions and assembling their forces. The following
spring they marched into Northumbria and took
possession of York. The Northumbrians made a
brave resistance, but the Danes defeated them again
and again. Ella, the King of Northumbria, was
taken prisoner, and the sons and friends of Ragnar
Lodbrog revenged themselves by putting his destroyer
to death with horrid tortures. The kingdom of
Northumbria was now overrun by the Northmen;
the sky was black with burning towns and villages,
and the air was filled with the lamentations of women
and children whose husbands and fathers had fallen
beneath the heavy axes of the Northmen.

To add to the misery which afflicted the Saxons,
a great dearth came upon the country, for the husbandmen could no longer till the ground in peace, and
the ploughshares had been exchanged for spears.

Alfred had now reached his nineteenth year, and
his brother, Ethelred, gave him a share in the kingly
dignity. In this year, 867, he married Ealswitha, the
daughter of a nobleman of Mercia. We do not know
much about this lady, but there is every reason to
believe that she proved a good and faithful wife, for
in Alfred's writings, which we can still read, he
describes with great feeling the joys of married life
and the comfort of a good wife in times of difficulty
and sorrow.

The ceremonies of the marriage lasted for four

days, but before they came to an end a circumstance occurred which filled the wedding guests with alarm. The young bridegroom was suddenly seized with an illness which caused him to suffer terrible agony. None of the Saxon physicians could discover the cause of this illness, or were able to cure it. It is probable, however, that it was a cancer in the stomach. This disease continued with Alfred until his death. His friend tells us that "if ever, by God's mercy, he was relieved from this infirmity for a single day or night, yet the fear and dread of that dreadful malady never left him, but rendered him almost useless, as he thought, for every duty, whether human or divine."

Nevertheless, in spite of this great affliction, Alfred proved a noble worker for the welfare of his country. Indeed, when we think of the life of danger and difficulty which he always led, the power of his enemies, the ignorance and superstition of his countrymen, and his continual suffering, we can only marvel that he should have become a distinguished scholar and the author of so many good works for the benefit of his people. Anyone afflicted by ill-health or surrounded with difficulty may take heart when he reads the life of Alfred the Great.

ALFRED'S FIRST ENCOUNTERS WITH THE DANES.

In the year following Alfred's marriage, the Northmen advanced into the kingdom of Mercia, and took possession of Nottingham. The Mercian king (who had married the sister of Ethelred and Alfred) urgently besought the King of Wessex to come to his aid. Ethelred was not indifferent to his brother-in-

law's danger, and he immediately joined the Mercians
with Alfred and a large force of West Saxons. After
besieging the Danish stronghold for some time, the
Saxons made a truce with their enemies The Northmen retreated to York, and Ethelred and Alfred
returned to Wessex.

The famine now increased to a fearful extent, so
that men and cattle died in great numbers. The
Northmen could obtain no advantages out of the
country's misery, and for a year they remained at
York.   In the following spring they broke forth
again, and from that time the kingdoms of Northumbria, East Anglia, and Mercia, experienced the fury
of the Northmen. Towns. villages, monasteries and
churches were delivered to the flames, while men,
women, and children, peaceful monks and helpless
nuns, were murdered with horrible cruelty.

At last, in the year 870, the Northmen advanced
into Wessex and took possession of the town of
Reading. In their first attempts to repel the invaders
the Saxons were defeated. Shortly afterwards, however, they succeeded in raising a larger and better
equipped army, and once more advanced to give
battle to the Danes. The struggle occurred at a place
called Æscesdun, or Ash-Tree Hill. The Danes had
gathered together all their forces, and they were
drawn up in two great bodies, one of which was led by
two kings, and the other by their earls.

Before the battle began King Ethelred remained
in his tent with a priest, and for a long time prayed
devoutly for divine aid that he might triumph over
his enemies in the coming battle. The Northmen
were already in battle array, and messengers were

sent to the king's tent requesting his presence at the head of the army. But Ethelred refused to leave his tent until he had finished his prayers. In the meanwhile the Northmen were preparing to advance. Alfred, impatient at his brother's delay, immediately led his troops against the foe. It is said that he attacked "like a chafed boar," but his boldness was not rewarded with success. The Danes had a superior position, for they were on a hill, and they drove the Saxons down with their mighty axes. Just as Alfred's force was falling back, Ethelred advanced at last with his reinforcements. The battle was again renewed with increased energy on the part of the Saxons, and after a long and desperate struggle the Danes fled in disorder, leaving thousands of dead upon the field. All through the night the English chased their enemies until they took refuge in their fortress at Reading.

This success of the West Saxons did not avail them much.

Another host of invaders now arrived from the North and increased the danger of the Saxons. They immediately joined their countrymen in Wessex, and two months after their arrival they inflicted a defeat upon the Saxons at Merton in Surrey. In this battle King Ethelred received a mortal wound, of which he died at Easter, in the year 871.

ALFRED BECOMES KING.

Ethelred left some children, but upon his death the earls and chiefs of the West Saxons, with the consent of the whole country, chose Alfred to be their king. We are told that the young prince hesitated to accept such a dangerous possession as the crown of Wessex, but he was induced to do so at the earnest entreaty of his countrymen.

At this time the Saxons were in despair. If they succeeded in defeating the invaders, fresh hordes poured over from the Baltic to fill up the gaps in the ranks of their countrymen. They came no longer to plunder and sail away, but they were determined to conquer the land and to found their kingdoms in it.

Alfred had hardly been king for a month when the Northmen inflicted a severe defeat upon his forces while he was absent. This was the ninth great battle which the West Saxons had fought during the year, besides a large number of small conflicts. The country was exhausted, and Alfred purchased a peace from his enemies, and induced them to retire to the northern counties of England.

For a short time the Northmen did not molest Wessex, but they overran the other parts of the country which could no longer offer a resistance. Alfred's brother-in-law deserted his kingdom of Mercia, and died an ignoble death at Rome. England was now divided among the Northmen and the Saxons, and the latter, who now only ruled in the kingdom of Wessex, awaited the moment when the hordes of barbarians should break the truce and advance in overwhelming numbers to attack them.

They did not have to wait long. In the following spring the Danes, commanded by their chief, Guthrun, left their winter quarters at Cambridge and began their attack upon the West Saxons. One night they sailed along the coast to Dorsetshire and captured the castle of Wareham. From this post of vantage they ravaged the neighbouring country with their usual cruelty. Alfred again offered them money to obtain peace. As before, the Danes took the money, and swore the most solemn oaths to keep the peace, but once again Alfred's faith in them was quickly disappointed. A few nights later th y rushed suddenly upon the Saxons and killed all their horsemen. Then they mounted the steeds of their victims and rode away to Exeter, where they passed the winter.

Alfred had now learnt the rapidity with which the Northmen moved from one part of the country to the other, and how they were constantly reinforced by fleets sailing across the English Channel. To encounter these difficulties he ordered a number of galleys, or long-ships, to be built at several ports in his kingdom. It was not long before his foresight was rewarded with success. The new Saxon vessels met a large Danish fleet sailing from a bay near Wareham to give assistance to their countrymen in another part of England. The Danish vessels had already been damaged in a heavy storm. Perceiving their advantage, the Saxon fleet attacked them fiercely, and when the battle ended, the Vikings and their crews were sent to the bottom of the sea, and one hundred and twenty of their "steeds of the ocean" (as they called their ships) were destroyed on the coast of Hampshire.

This was the first time that an English fleet defended our shores from foreign invasion. King Alfred may be called the Father of the English Navy, for he was the first to discover that as long as his countrymen could defend the English Channel the shores of England would be protected from the attack of foreign invaders. Alfred's first naval victory could not crush the overwhelming numbers of his enemies, and, as we shall see, he lost his kingdom for a time; but in after years, when he had regained it, he built many ships, and it was chiefly owing to the strength of his navy that he was able to defend his country from invaders.

Shortly after Alfred's victory at sea, fresh swarms of "the Locusts of the Baltic" landed in Northumbria, and, having joined their countrymen, who were already masters of the northern counties of England, advanced into Wessex. The Saxons now fell into despair, and many of them fled over the sea to France and other countries. The rest submitted to the Northmen, and at last Alfred himself, deserted by his people, and powerless against his enemies, was forced to fly for his life, and to take refuge in the wild marshes of Somerset.

ALFRED AT ATHELNEY.

An old Saxon writer says that when the Danish army approached "he took flight, and went hiding over hedges and ways, woods and wilds, till, through the divine guidance, he came to the Isle of Athelney."

Athelney, which means "the isle of nobles," is a district in the low-lying country of Somerset, surrounded by marshes and bounded by the rivers Parrett and Tone. In Alfred's time it could only be approached by boats, and was covered with a great wood in which lived stags and goats and many other animals.

Alfred fled alone to this place, which he had

probably visited before on one of his hunting expeditions. He took refuge in the hut of a cowherd,
who lived in this lonely spot with his wife. The poor
couple did not know that the man who begged for
shelter was their king, but they were moved with pity
and supplied him with food and a resting place.

Alfred remained with these people for some days.
The story is told that one day, as he sat by the hearth
mending his bow and thinking with a sad heart of
the misery of his country, the cowherd's wife put
some loaves to cook on a pan, with fire underneath,
and asked Alfred to mind them for her. But Alfred's
thoughts were busy with other matters, and when the
woman happened, in a little while, to glance at her
loaves she found them burning on one side. An old
chronicler who tells the story says :

'She immediately assailed the king with reproaches. 'Why, man! do you sit thinking there,
and are too proud to turn the bread ? Whatever be
your family, with such manners and sloth, what
trust can be put in you hereafter ? If you were even
a nobleman, you will be glad to eat the bread which
you neglect to attend to.' The king, though stung by
her upbraidings, yet heard her with patience and
mildness, and, roused by her scolding, took care to
bake the bread as she wished."

One day, while Alfred was at Athelney, he was
recognised by some of his nobles, who were flying
from the Danes. They joined him eagerly, and the
king, who had recovered from his despair, consulted
them how they might best make a stand against
their enemies. They were soon joined by other
Saxon nobles and warriors, and under the direction of

the king they fortified themselves in the little island.
Here they led an adventurous life for many months.
The only food they could obtain was by hunting or
fishing, and they often suffered from hunger.

Whenever Alfred learnt that the Danes were in
his neighbourhood he would start from the island
with his little band of warriors, and, taking the enemy
by surprise, attack them with great energy and
courage. If he met with a superior force, he would
retire to his island-retreat as speedily as he had
darted upon his foes, who were bewildered and
terrified. "By day and night, at dawn, in the evening
twilight, from woods and marshes, he was ever
rushing on the Northmen." We are told that "the
king, both when he failed and when he was successful,
preserved a cheerful countenance, and supported his
friends by his example." By these means Alfred
gained great experience as a soldier and a thorough
knowledge of the country, and he learnt the position
of his enemies. He also put new heart into his
countrymen, who heard of his deeds with joy and
renewed hope.

Alfred passed six months in the island of
Athelney. At the end of that time he determined to
make a great effort to gather together a large force
of Saxons, and to surprise the main army of the
Northmen who were stationed at Eddington, near
Westbury, in Wiltshire.

Some of the old chroniclers relate that Alfred
resolved to visit the Danish camp himself, in order
to discover its force and position. As we have
already said, he had a great fondness for Saxon
poetry, and was also a good musician upon the

harp. Disguised as a harper, he visited the Danish camp and gained the applause of the Northmen by his singing and music. He was admitted to the table of Guthrum, the king, and listened to his conversation with his warriors. Having gained a great deal of useful information, he then left the Danish camp, and returned in safety to his family and friends at Athelney.

He now sent messengers to all parts of Wessex, summoning his friends to join him secretly with as many followers as they could muster. The meeting was arranged to take place at a celebrated spot called Egbert's Stone, in Selwood Forest. Many of the Saxons had abandoned hope of regaining their country from the Danes, and they believed Alfred to be dead, but when they heard that he was going to lead them once more against their enemies they were filled with gladness, and marched eagerly to the appointed place.

A GREAT VICTORY.

Two days passed while the Saxon warriors assembled in Selwood Forest, and greeted their king with acclamation. At last, on the third day, Alfred marched with his new army to a place called Ecglea (the Field of Oaks) and surveyed the enemy from a hill. The following morning they advanced rapidly towards Eddington, where the Northmen were stationed in great numbers.

Alfred then halted and formed his army in battle array. Before leading them against the enemy he spoke a few stirring words to them. He reminded them that they were going to fight for their wives and

children, for their country, and for their lives. He
urged them to act like brave men, and he promised
them a glorious victory. Then he signed to them to
follow him and to advance upon their enemies.

The Anglo-Saxons dashed upon the Danes in a

Photo: E. Wilkinson, Trowbridge.

THE WHITE HORSE BETWEEN DIDCOT AND SWINDON.

disciplined array, and with a fierce courage which the
Northmen could not withstand. Alfred himself led
them on, and the presence of their king inspired the
Saxons with an enthusiasm which swept all before
them like pebbles before the sea. Having let fly a
storm of arrows, they charged with their lances, and
finally they came to close quarters with their swords.

The Danes, who had been taken by surprise, defended themselves with their usual courage, but fell like straw to the sickle before the Saxon swords. The plain was strewn with Danes, dying and dead, and, at last, the remnants of their great army fled with their king to a neighbouring fortification. Here Alfred besieged them for fourteen days, until, exhausted by fighting and hunger, the Danish chiefs laid down their arms and humbly begged for peace and mercy.

ALFRED'S JEWEL.

By this victory Alfred, who had been a half-starved fugitive in the island of Athelney, regained his kingdom, and the Danes received a greater defeat than they had suffered for twelve years.

On the hills between Didcot and Swindon may be seen the figure of a white horse, cut out of the chalk. It is supposed that this horse was made to commemorate the great battle of Eddington, and that ever since it has been preserved and kept free from grass by the inhabitants of the neighbourhood. There is another relic which still remains to remind us of the days when Alfred was concealed in the marshes of Athelney. In the Ashmolean Museum, at Oxford, there is a jewel beautifully worked in gold, which was found at Athelney. It bears the words ".Elfred mec heht gewyrean" (Alfred had me made).

Alfred not only granted pardon to the Danes, but he offered them the undisturbed possession of East Anglia on the condition that they would settle down peacefully in that district and adopt the Christian religion. Guthrum, the Danish chief, accepted these conditions, and a week later he was baptised, receiving the name of Ethelstan, and his conqueror, Alfred, as his godfather. He remained twelve days with the king, and at his departure he was presented with magnificent gifts.

The conversion of the Danish chief to Christianity must have been in name only, but it is pleasant to learn that he kept to his promises, and his countrymen remained peaceably in the district which Alfred had given to them. This district contained the counties of Norfolk, Suffolk, Cambridge, and small portions of Essex, Hertford, Bedford, and Huntingdon. In these counties at the present day there are many Danish names of villages, streams, and hills, and many of the inhabitants are descended from those old Vikings who proved such fierce enemies of the Anglo-Saxons.

Alfred's first care after his restoration was to fortify the country against the attacks of Northern invaders. He rebuilt castles and towns which had been destroyed by the Danes, and made new fortifications in numerous parts of the country. He also caused many ships of war to be built according to his own designs, and he encouraged the Anglo-Saxons to exercise themselves in the art of navigation. By these wise preparations he was able to defeat several fleets of Northmen who came over to England a few years after his great victory. When they found that the country was so well defended, and not receiving any assistance from their countrymen in East Anglia they sailed away to France and other countries, where they hoped to obtain plunder more easily.

ALFRED'S LONG PEACE.

For nearly fifteen years Alfred was now left in the peaceful possession of his kingdom. He spent these years with untiring industry for the welfare of his people and for the benefit of future generations of Englishmen.

One of his greatest desires was to obtain the education which had been denied to him in the years of his youth. He invited the most learned men of his kingdom to his court, and they were never weary of teaching such an eager and industrious pupil. Werfrith, the Bishop of Worcester, and Plegmund, the Archbishop of Canterbury, were among those who were his first teachers. We are told that by day and night, whenever he could find the leisure to listen, they recited or interpreted the books he wished to master. In this way, although he was still unable to read Latin, he obtained a knowledge of what the books contained. The more he learned, however, the more he was eager to know, and he sent abroad for learned men who would be willing to teach him. In this way he obtained Grimbald, the priest whom he had met years ago upon his journey to Rome. This man was renowned for his great learning and for his beautiful character. Another of Alfred's teachers was John the Irishman, a monk skilled in many arts, familiar with many languages, and with the masterpieces of Latin literature. With these companions Alfred studied the Scriptures, and works of philosophy, history, and travel, by Latin authors, which they interpreted for him into Saxon. In return for these services he rewarded his teachers with magnificent liberality.

The king then came to hear of the merit of Asser, the Bishop of St. Davids, in Wales. " I was called by the king," relates this worthy Saxon, " from the western extremities of Wales I accompanied my conductors to Sussex, and first saw him in the royal city of Dene. I was benignantly received by him. Amongst other conversation, he asked me earnestly to devote myself to his service, and to become his companion." Asser did not accept the king's offer for some time, but at length, after some persuasion to leave his friends in Wales, he took up his abode at the king's court.

It was chiefly owing to Asser that Alfred was at last able to learn Latin. Asser was in the habit of quoting wise sentences from the Latin authors, and then translating them into Saxon for the benefit of the king. One day Alfred was struck with one of these quotations, and, taking from his bosom a little book of devotions, he requested Asser to write down the sentence in it. Asser, however, suggested that they should put a few blank pages together, in order that they might put down any other quotations that pleased the king. Alfred agreed to this pro- posal, and soon the leaves were full of Latin quota- tions which Alfred learnt by heart. He took a great delight in this little " manual," and kept it with him upon all occasions. By degrees he became acquainted with a great deal of Latin, and with the help of his friend Asser he at last obtained a thorough knowledge of that language.

No sooner did he possess this knowledge than he was eager to devote it to the education of his people. The Saxons were mostly ignorant and coarse, and Alfred wisely considered that the best way to improve their condition was to educate them. He immediately set himself to work to translate a number of Latin books into the Saxon language, and to establish schools, so that, in his own words, "all the youth that are now in England who are free men, and have so much wealth as may satisfy themselves, be committed to learning, so that for a time they may apply to no other duty till they first well know to read English writing. Let them learn further the Latin language, they who will further learn, and will advance to a higher education."

Among the works which Alfred translated into the Saxon language were "The Consolations of Philosophy," by Boethius, "A History of the World," by Orosius, and "A History of the Anglo-Saxon Nation," which had been written in Latin by a learned Saxon priest, named the Venerable Bede. Another important work which Alfred translated was a book by Gregory, the Pope who sent over St. Augustine to England to convert the Saxons to Christianity. He also translated some of the Psalms of David and several old Latin stories.

In many of these works Alfred did not translate the original author word for word, but he added his own thoughts upon the subjects dealt with. It is from these books, as well as from the story of his life by Asser and the old chroniclers, that we can become acquainted with Alfred's character.

Anyone who reads the following sentences, which are Alfred's own words, must admire the wisdom and beautiful character of the man who wrote them.

WISE WORDS OF ALFRED THE GREAT.

"This is clear enough, that a good word and good fame are better and more precious to every man than any riches."

"Learn, therefore, wisdom, and when ye have learned it, do not neglect it. I tell you, then, without any doubt, that by that you may come to *power*, though you should not desire the power, nor strive after it. If you be wise and good, it will follow you, though you should not wish it."

"We too much undervalue ourselves when we love that which is inferior to us."

"*Covetousness* maketh the avaricious odious both to God and man, while *bounty* maketh us always pleasing and famous, and worthy both to God and to men who love it."

"Oh, glory of the world! Why do silly men with a false voice call thee glory? Now thou art not so; for more men have much pomp and much glory, and much worship from the opinion of foolish people, than they have from their own works."

"Behold now the spaciousness and the constancy and the swiftness of the heavens! Yet we may understand that all this is not to be compared with its Creator and its Governor. . . . Every existence is to be honoured according to its · position, and always the highest first. Therefore the Divine power is to be honoured, admired and worshipped above all other existences."

"True friends! I say then that this is the most precious of all the riches of the world. They are not even to be reckoned among the goods of the word, but as *divine* ones, because false fortune can neither bring them nor take them away."

Alfred was so anxious that the important offices of the kingdom should be filled by men who were capable of undertaking them that he compelled them to study literature, willy nilly. Even the nobles who had reached an advanced age without being able to read or write were obliged to begin to learn. If they were too old to master the difficulties of reading and writing, their son or kinsman, or some freeman or slave, was educated for the purpose of reciting Saxon books before the ignorant noblemen.

In spite of this severity, Asser tells us that Alfred " was affable and pleasant to all, and curiously eager to investigate things unknown. Many Franks, Frisians, Gauls, Pagans, Britons, Scots and Armoricans, noble and ignoble, submitted voluntarily to his dominion, and all of them according to their nation and deserving were honoured, and enriched with money and power. . . . His bishops, too, and all ecclesiastics, his earls, nobles, ministers and friends were loved by him with wonderful affection, and their sons who were bred up in the royal household were no less dear to him than his own ; he had them instructed in all kinds of good morals, and among other things never ceased to teach them letters night and day."

Alfred set a noble example to his countrymen in the first duty of all parents—that is, in the education of their families. Alfred's children were brought up with great care. They were taught to give strict obedience to their parents, and to be gentle and affable to everyone they met. They were encouraged to spend their days to advantage by gaining as much knowledge as possible. They were also carefully instructed in Saxon and Latin books, and especially in Saxon poetry. When they were sufficiently advanced in age their bodies were exercised with the same care as their minds, and they were encouraged to take part in all the out-of-door sports of their countrymen.

Some of Alfred's final instructions to his son have been recorded, and they are examples of his piety and wisdom, and of his anxiety for the welfare of his people.

"I pray thee (for thou art my dear child) strive to be a father and a lord to thy people. Be thou the children's father and the widow's friend. Comfort thou the poor and shelter the weak, and with all thy might right that which is wrong. And, son, govern thyself, by law: then shall the Lord love thee, and God above all things shall be thy reward."

With the help of his councillors Alfred made a code, or collection of laws. Many of these were his own, while others were selected from the laws established by his ancestors. He put them into writing and showed them to all the officers of his kingdom, who agreed that they should henceforth be obeyed.

Alfred not only *made* the laws of his kingdom, but he also *administered* them. It is said that the

rules of justice were so little understood at that time
that the nobles and even the common people would
quarrel angrily before their judges. Nor would they
willingly accept any judgment, save from the king
himself. Alfred was so anxious that complete justice
should be given to all, that he examined many of
these disputes himself with great patience and
industry. If he found that the judges had given
a wrong decision, we are told that he reproved them
mildly, and inquired into the reasons of their error.
If they would not accept his reproof in a respectful
manner, he addressed them in some such words as
the following:

"I wonder truly at your insolence, that whereas
by God's favour and mine you have occupied the
rank and office of the wise. Either, therefore, give
up the discharge of the temporal duties which you
hold, or endeavour more zealously to study the
lessons of wisdom. Such are my commands."

In this way Alfred laboured for the welfare of his
people. He was especially anxious to improve the
condition of the poor, and amongst his multitude of
other duties he constantly endeavoured to carry out
this desire.

"In all his kingdom," says Asser, "the poor had
no helpers, or very few, besides him. The rich and
powerful, engrossed with their own concerns, were
inattentive to their inferiors. They studied their
private, not the public good"

ALFRED'S LAST YEARS.

Towards the end of his reign Alfred was suddenly called from his peaceful labours to defend his

kingdom, once again, from "the Locusts of the Baltic."

In the year 893, Hastings, a Viking famous for his courage and military genius, sailed from the North, in command of two hundred and fifty vessels, to the south-west coast of Kent. The Northmen landed near Romney Marsh and captured a fortification, from which point they spread into Hampshire and Berkshire, burning, killing, and plundering.

Alfred raised an army and rapidly advanced towards his enemy, fully prepared to do battle. Hastings, who had never met with such an organised resistance, entrenched himself in a strong position and erected fortifications, so that Alfred would not hazard an attack.

Alfred's plan was to surround the Danes with an overwhelming force, so that they would have to submit or perish. This plan, however, required time, and the Saxon army was chiefly composed of husbandmen who could not be absent from their farms all through the year. To do away with this difficulty, Alfred divided his army into two bodies one of which was called to the war while the men in the other division were peaceably tilling their fields. After a few months' service the warriors returned home, while the husbandmen took their places. In this way Alfred was able to keep an army always confronting the enemy.

After a while the Danes grew tired of keeping within their entrenchments, and they ventured out to fight the Saxons. In their first battle they were heavily defeated, but Hastings was a man of genius, far superior to Alfred's old enemy, Guthrun. No

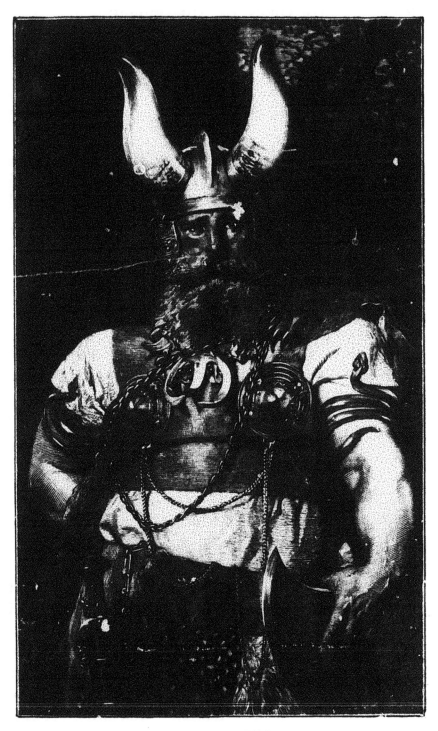

A VIKING CHIEF.

(By permission, from the picture by Carl Haag, R.W.S.)

sooner was he defeated in one place than he moved rapidly to another part of the country to plunder and destroy. He was supported, also, by another fleet of Northmen, who came to share his battles and his plunder.

Alfred watched the movements of his enemies with untiring vigilance, and followed the foe up and down the country. He defeated them again and again, on land and sea, but after each defeat they appeared in some other quarter, with fresh recruits and with the same fierce courage.

For three years Hastings struggled fiercely against Alfred's skill and wisdom. At last, worn out with fighting and with an army greatly reduced by numerous defeats, he saw that fortune was against him, and he set sail from England with the remnants of his force.

He left England in peace, but for many years it bore the traces of his ravages and destruction. The miseries of the war were surpassed by the misfortune which afflicted the country upon its conclusion. A fearful plague broke out, and for three years it spread death throughout the land, and both the nobles and the poor were struck down in great numbers.

The remainder of Alfred's days were now filled with peaceful work for his people. He strengthened the defence of his country by having new ships built according to his own improved designs, and he repaired or rebuilt towns, castles and monasteries which had been destroyed by the Danes. He continued his labours for the education of his people, and he gave charity or advice to all who were in need of it. At last, on the 26th of October, in the year 901, the good king died, beloved by all his people after a life spent in splendid work.

His character is expressed in the noble words which he has left as an example to every citizen of the British Empire:

"This I can now most truly say, that I have desired to live worthily while I lived, and after my life to leave to the men that should be after me my remembrance in good works."

The names by which the Anglo-Saxons called King Alfred show how much he was reverenced and beloved by his people. They called him "Alfred the Truth-teller," "England's Comfort," and "England's Darling." People of our own time justly call him "Alfred the Great."

II.

STEPHEN LANGTON

AND THE GREAT CHARTER.

THE name of Stephen Langton should always be connected, in the minds of Englishmen, with that great charter of English rights which will ever be famous by the name of *Magna Charta*. It was Stephen Langton who drew up this charter to protect the liberties of his countrymen from the tyranny of an unjust king, and it was chiefly owing to his patriotism and courage that King John was forced to make all the good promises which the charter contains.

This great Englishman was born in the year 1151. Unfortunately, we possess no information about his early years, except that he was the son of noble and wealthy parents, and that he received a good education. When he became a young man he went to the University of Paris, which at that time was the most famous place of learning in Europe. Here he distinguished himself as a poet and a scholar.

At this time he became acquainted with a man who was to have a great influence upon his future life, an Italian of noble family named Lothaire. He was a man of remarkable talent and unbounded charity. Stephen Langton was also renowned for his pious character, and these two men soon became dear and intimate friends. When Lothaire afterwards became head of the Christian Church, under the title of Pope Innocent III., he still kept up his friendship with Stephen Langton. It was not long, indeed, before he summoned him to Rome, and made him a cardinal.

At this time King John was on the throne of England, and when the news came that Stephen Langton had been made a cardinal he wrote a letter of warm congratulation to him. It was not long, however, before an event happened which turned the king's friendly sentiments into fierce hatred.

THE CHOOSING OF AN ARCHBISHOP.

Hubert, the Archbishop of Canterbury, died, and it was necessary to choose another man to fill his place. Of course, as the office of archbishop was the most important in the English Church, it was necessary that a man right good and worthy should be found to fill it, and that much careful consideration should be given to the matter. In spite of this, however, a number of young monks of Christchurch, Canterbury, were in a great hurry to choose their new archbishop. They elected one of their superiors, named Reginald, and, without waiting for the consent of the Pope, or the king, which was really required, they sent Reginald to Rome to be formally installed as archbishop. We are told that Reginald was a vulgar, conceited, foolish man. He arrived in Rome with great pomp and parade, and made himself so ridiculous that Pope Innocent wisely refused to make him Archbishop of Canterbury.

In the meantime King John was furious because

the monks of Canterbury had chosen a person to
be archbishop without his consent. He refused to
agree to their choice, and forthwith chose one of
his favourites, named John de Grey, Bishop of
Norwich. The king forgot, however, that it was

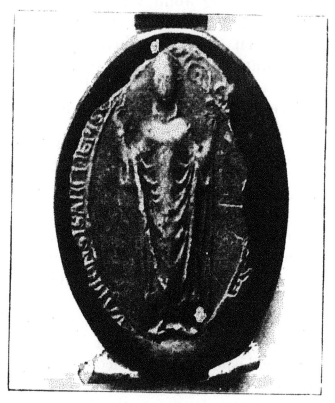

A SEAL OF STEPHEN LANGTON.

necessary to get the Pope's consent, and he was
very angry and indignant when Pope Innocent
rejected John de Grey in the same manner that he
had done Reginald.

The Pope, as the head of the Church, could
choose whom he liked to be archbishop, and he
therefore elected his friend Stephen Langton, whom

he considered to be the wisest and best man to fill
the office of Archbishop of Canterbury.

THE KING'S FURY.

There is no doubt that the Pope's choice was
the best, but King John thought otherwise. He
got into a terrible fury, and refused to admit the
new archbishop into his kingdom. He threw the
Pope's messengers into prison, and when the monks
of Canterbury obeyed the Pope's wishes to recognise
Stephen as the archbishop he drove them out of
the country.

Pope Innocent now threatened to lay England
under an interdict unless King John admitted
Archbishop Stephen into his kingdom. To lay a
country under an interdict meant in those days to
deprive it of all religious services. The churches
were all closed, the dead could not be buried in a
Christian manner, and the people remained without
any of the consolations of religion.

The clergy, the barons, and the people of England
naturally dreaded that such a state of things should
come about. They came to the king and implored
him to give way to the Pope. But John would
not yield. He swore by a terrible oath that if Pope
Innocent dared to lay his kingdom under an interdict
he would chase all the churchmen out of England
and seize their property. He promised also that
if any of the clergy of the Church of Rome were
to be found in England he would send them back
to Rome with their eyes plucked out and their
noses slit.

Pope Innocent was not frightened by John's

brutal threats, and proceeded to lay the kingdom under an interdict. On the appointed day the churches of England were closed, the bells ceased to ring, and no service was celebrated. For more than two years this terrible state of things prevailed in England, and still John stubbornly refused to yield. At last, however, he realised that he would have to submit or lose his kingdom. He was surrounded by enemies. The clergy, the barons, and the people hated him for his tyranny, and for the misery he had brought upon them. In addition to enemies at home, he now saw himself threatened by enemies abroad, for the Pope had requested the King of France to invade England in order to dethrone such an abominable king as John. With secret rage and terror, John at length submitted to the Pope, to the great joy of the whole kingdom. At last the miseries of the interdict were removed, and now for the first time Archbishop Langton was able to exercise the duties of the office to which he had been appointed.

THE KING'S PENITENCE.

When the archbishop arrived at Dover, he was informed that the king was at Cranborne, in Wiltshire. After communications had passed between the king and the archbishop, it was arranged that they should meet one another at Winchester.

On the Feast of St. Margaret, July 20th, 1214, Archbishop Stephen, surrounded by an imposing cavalcade of churchmen, halted on the lovely downs which surround the old city of Winchester. Presently they caught sight of a procession of barons and knights in bright-coloured garments, with brilliant banners fluttering in the breeze, slowly issuing from the city gate. The archbishop and his attendants soon perceived that it was the king surrounded by his courtiers who were approaching them. As the procession came nearer, Archbishop Stephen hesitated how to receive the king who had so long been his bitter enemy. His doubts, however, were at an end when King John stepped ahead of his courtiers, and cast himself prostrate at the feet of the archbishop. When we know John's deceitful and immoral character, we cannot help thinking that this humility and contrition must have been false. The archbishop, however, was profoundly touched by these signs of penitence from one whom he had hitherto regarded as an obstinate sinner. He burst into tears and raised the king from the ground. The churchmen and the courtiers now formed into one procession, and they followed the king and the archbishop into the city, chanting the Fifty-first Psalm.

The multitude of people waiting round Winchester Cathedral were filled with astonishment and delight when they saw the procession enter the cathedral. More joyous were they still when the king swore solemnly before the altar that he would govern the country according to the good old laws of King Edward the Confessor, which had been adopted by King Henry I. and other succeeding sovereigns.

Archbishop Stephen began his new duties with high hope that the king would amend his evil ways. He soon learnt, however, with sorrow, that all John's solemn promises were no sooner made than broken.

King John was perhaps the worst king that has ever sat upon the English throne. There is little doubt that he was the murderer of his nephew Arthur: he robbed his people of their hard-earned money; he imprisoned them unlawfully; he brought over foreign favourites, to whom he gave castles and lands which rightfully belonged to his English nobles; he refused to obey the orders of the Church, and, indeed, he broke almost every law of God and man. For these offences all classes of the English people—the barons, the clergy, and the citizens—regarded him with an intense hatred.

Stephen Langton, being the head of the Church in England, was not a man who would tamely sit still while the laws of that Church were being trampled upon. He had also a stout English heart which bade him defend the liberties of his country-men against the brutal injustice of a tyrant. King John soon found to his cost that the new archbishop was a man of high principle and unflinching courage.

THE GREAT COUNCIL.

In the summer of 1214 the king summoned a great council of barons and clergy to discuss the affairs of the kingdom, but, without waiting to attend it himself, he set out on an expedition to France, and left one of his barons, Geoffrey Fitzwalter, to govern the country during his absence.

The council met at St. Albans on the 4th of August, 1214. The barons and clergy attended full of angry determination to take measures to check the king's evil doings. The pious, brave, and patriotic Archbishop Stephen was the spokesman of their grievances. Acting upon his advice, the Great Council made a solemn resolution that the laws of the king's grandfather, Henry I., should be obeyed by king and people. Then they issued orders to all the king's officers—who had made themselves hated for their cruelty and robbery—requiring them, at the peril of life and limb, to abstain from taking the people's money unjustly, and from all acts of violence and oppression which they had hitherto done without hindrance.

It was all very well, however, to say that the laws of King Henry I. should be obeyed, but King John had governed so long without any laws at all that the barons and clergy were in some doubt as to what the laws were, and where they could be found.

Archbishop Stephen, with his usual good sense, determined to solve the difficulty, and he ordered thorough search to be made for the old laws. It was soon found that copies had been sent to every county and placed in all the monastic libraries. They were the old Saxon laws, known as the laws of Edward the Confessor, which had been written down by some of the Saxon kings such as Alfred and Edward the Confessor. When the Norman kings, William the Conqueror and his son Rufus, had come to the English throne, the old Saxon laws were not formally adopted, although many of them still remained in force. When, however, the first Henry succeeded to the crown, he caused the old Saxon laws to be solemnly proclaimed as the laws

D

of the land, and he granted a charter to the English people in which he promised that he and his descendants would always obey the laws. King Stephen and Henry II. also promised to maintain those laws, and although they did not always keep their promises, yet the laws remained a warning to these despotic kings, and the rights of the English people were clearly stated in them.

The council of St. Albans was broken up while search was being made for the old laws. It met again shortly afterwards at St. Paul's Cathedral. King John was still away from his kingdom, but a great gathering of nobles and knights, bishops, abbots, and priors assembled to discuss public affairs.

Archbishop Stephen was once again the leading spirit in this assembly. He took advantage of the opportunity to encourage the barons to unite in the defence of the liberties of the country.

"Did you hear," he said, "how, when I absolved the king at Winchester, I made him swear that he would do away with unjust laws, and would recall good laws such as those of King Edward, and cause them to be observed by all in the kingdom? A charter of Henry I., King of England, has just now been found, by which you may, if you wish it, recall your long-lost rights and your former condition."

Thereupon the archbishop read out the charter in which King Henry had solemnly promised that he and his descendants would obey the Saxon laws.

While the archbishop read out this charter, a deep silence fell upon the vast assembly of barons and clergy. They listened eagerly to the words which spoke of those English liberties and rights

which had been so outraged by King John. Every
now and again a baron would show his excitement
by grasping the handle of his sword, or by a muttered
exclamation. When the archbishop had finished
reading, a mighty burst of applause broke out among
the nobles and knights, and with loud shouts they
made known their readiness to fight and, if need be,
to die for their rights.

"Swear it!" cried the archbishop, facing the excited
assembly with flashing eyes and outstretched hands.

In a moment the hand of every baron and knight
was stretched towards Heaven, and, as if with one
voice, they shouted, "We swear!"

The solemn words echoed and re-echoed down
the aisles of old St. Paul's, and when they faded
away into silence the barons stood pledged to resist
the tyranny of King John to the very death. It
was this promise which gained for Englishmen of
those days and for ourselves that great charter
which is still the pride of the English nation.

Not long after this event, the king hurried back
to England, thoroughly alarmed by the news which
had reached him concerning the councils of St. Albans
and St. Paul's. He found the barons arming themselves as if to prepare for war. John did not number
cowardice among his vices, and he immediately set
to work to endeavour to raise an army sufficiently
strong to put down his rebellious barons. As yet
he had no intention of submitting to them. He
openly proclaimed that "he hated like viper's blood
the noblemen of rank in the kingdom, especially
Sayer de Quincey, Robert Fitzwalter, and Stephen,
Archbishop of Canterbury."

THE GREAT CHARTER.

Archbishop Stephen did not quail before the king's hatred. On the contrary, he paid a visit with a retinue of priests to the king's camp at Northampton. There, calmly and fearlessly, he stated that he came to remind the king of that oath he had made at Winchester when he had promised solemnly to govern rightly and justly according to the law of the land. Then he pointed to the king's small army opposed to the power and determination of the barons. He told the king that every baron had made an oath that he would no longer serve him if he refused to grant the old English rights, and that they would wage war against him until by charter **under his** seal the king confirmed their just demands.

When Archbishop Stephen finished speaking, the king broke out into a furious rage.

" Why do you not demand my crown at once ? " he shouted. Then, swearing a horrible oath, he cried, " No liberties will I grant to those whose object it is to make me a slave."

But King John soon realised that his **rage was** of no avail against the determination of Archbishop Stephen and the barons. One by one his followers left him, and he saw his army dwindle into an insignificant force. At last he was obliged to promise that he would fix a time in which to meet his barons and hear their grievances.

In April of the year 1215 the barons assembled in full force at Stamford. From all parts of the kingdom they came with their retainers fully armed and burning with enthusiasm to defend their rights which had been trodden under foot by **the king.**

KING JOHN SIGNING MAGNA CHARTA.

Two thousand knights were there, in complete armour, with their cavalry, infantry, and attendants. It must have been a glorious sight when the April sun shone down on the glittering armour, the waving plumes, the bright banners, the tall lances and the gleaming swords of those English warriors, who called themselves "The Army of God and the Holy Church." Each man was ready to uphold the liberty of England with the strength of his sword. Each man was eager to face the fury of John.

By this time King John was deserted by almost everybody in the kingdom. It is said, indeed, that only seven knights remained with him. He saw, therefore, that he was powerless in the hands of his barons, and he agreed to meet them wherever they chose.

The famous meeting took place in a broad and smooth meadow on the banks of the Thames, about three miles from Windsor bridge. The barons proceeded to the meadow from Staines, and the king came from Windsor. In this field, called Runnymede, King John was forced to listen while Magna Charta, the great charter of English liberty, was read out to him for the first time by Stephen Langton, the archbishop. He was surrounded by armed warriors who had sworn to fight and, if need be, die in the defence of their rights. John was powerless, and on June 15th, 1215, in the meadow of Runnymede, Magna Charta was signed and sealed, and became the law of the land.

THE MEANING OF MAGNA CHARTA.

In this way, Stephen Langton and the barons of England obtained the famous charter of English rights called Magna Charta.

It would be well for every Englishman to know the use and contents of the charter.

In the first place, it is necessary to remember that Archbishop Stephen and his friends did not invent a number of new laws which they forced the king to sign. What they did was to write down the old English laws and customs which the king had so shamefully disregarded, and which they desired him to observe in the future.

Magna Charta was written in Latin, and contained forty-nine articles, or clauses. Many of these articles had to do with the old "feudal law," which was then the law of the land. This law related chiefly to the duties of the barons to the king, and those of the common people to the barons, in time of war, and to other old customs which have long ago passed away. For this reason many of the articles in Magna Charta are no longer important at the present day. There are others, however, which are just as important now as they were in the time of King John, and they still form part of the English laws by which Englishmen are governed at the present day.

Chief among these is Article 40 of the Great Charter :

"*To none will we sell, to none will we refuse, to none will we deny Right and Justice.*"

Some readers perhaps may not understand at once the great importance of this promise, but a few words will explain this. "We" in the above sentence means the king, and in these words he promised not to *sell* Right and Justice. This promise was very necessary in the time of **King**

John, for he had often caused judgment to be given in favour of persons who paid him money for it, so that a guilty person could escape punishment if he were rich, while innocent persons often suffered because they were poor.

When the king signed Magna Charta, he promised not to *delay* justice. This also was necessary, for, often, persons desiring justice had been obliged to wait many weary years, and even their whole lifetime, without obtaining it. King John also promised that justice should never be *refused* to rich or poor, noble or peasant.

If John and the kings that came after him had kept this splendid promise written down in Magna Charta, the history of England would be very different from what it now is. Many unjust wars would have been avoided, many persons wrongfully imprisoned or wrongfully executed would have lived in peace and comfort, and the long story of bloodshed, wickedness, and suffering which darkens the pages of English history would have remained untold. Unfortunately, King John and other English kings did not respect their most solemn promises, and the laws written down in Magna Charta were often disregarded because the English people were not strong or bold enough to protect their rights. Nevertheless, when kings ignored the liberties and rights of the English people, they knew they were offending against Magna Charta, which they had promised to obey, and when the people were bold enough to resist the tyranny of unjust kings they could point to Magna Charta to show that they were only defending the law of England.

When Magna Charta was first signed by King John, many copies of it were made and sent to different parts of the country. In the British Museum the original copy is still to be seen, stained and faded by time. It bears the signature and seal of King John. There are few people who can look upon this old parchment without emotion when they think that, to uphold the promises written upon it, many of the best and bravest Englishmen suffered, fought, and died.

THE AUTHOR OF MAGNA CHARTA.

To Stephen Langton, Archbishop of Canterbury, we owe in a large measure the signing of Magna Charta. He did not, however, gain any earthly reward for his patriotism and bravery, but, on the contrary, he suffered exile and disgrace.

As soon as King John had signed the Great Charter, he sent messengers to Pope Innocent at Rome, mis-stating the facts and urging the Pope to condemn the Charter. The Pope was deceived by the king's statements, and condemned the barons for what he considered was an unlawful rebellion against their king. He ordered Archbishop Langton to excommunicate (that is to say, *to cut off from the Church*) any barons who would not submit to the king. But when Stephen refused to do so the Pope forbade him to continue his duties as Archbishop of Canterbury. Stephen Langton went to Rome himself, to persuade his old friend to recognise the justice of his conduct, but King John had so thoroughly misinformed the Pope that Stephen Langton was unable to convince him of the truth.

For the remainder of John's reign, the brave and patriotic Englishman continued to be an exile from his country. When King John's death in 1216 relieved England from his vice and tyranny, Langton was permitted to return and resume his government as Archbishop of Canterbury. The last years of his life were spent in quiet but constant work for the good of the Church, the relief of the poor, and the education of the English people in the knowledge of God.

Shortly before his death, in 1228, he retired to the Manor House in the little village of Slindon, in Sussex, and his last days were spent in peaceful retirement.

An old chronicler records his death in the following words:

"In XI. yere of Henry, deied Stevene Langdon, Bishop of Cauntirbury, that was a grete cleike in his days in making of many bokes, specially upon Scripture."

It is believed that Stephen Langton was the first to divide the Bible into chapters. The name, however, of the brave, good, and patriotic Englishman will always be remembered best in connection with the great record of English rights, called Magna Charta.

III.

SIMON DE MONTFORT

AND

THE RISE OF THE ENGLISH PARLIAMENT.

Almost every Englishman has a share in the government of his country. That is to say, that Englishmen have the right to take part in the election of members of Parliament, who are largely responsible for the proper government of their country. As they represent the opinions of the people who have chosen them, it is clear that the people themselves have a real share in their own government. This is certainly right and just, for if the people of England obey the laws, it is only fair that they should have a share in the making of them: and as they supply the money necessary for the public expenses of the country, they have a right to see that it is spent in a proper manner.

English citizens are nowadays so used to choosing members to represent their wishes in Parliament that they are apt to forget that their countrymen have not always had this right, and that it required much hard fighting on the part of brave Englishmen to win this privilege for themselves and their descendants.

To Simon de Montfort more than to any other man we owe our Parliament, and for this reason every Englishman should honour his memory. Although a foreigner by birth, he became an Englishman at heart, and the best years of his life were spent in

defending the English people from the tyrannies of
their king. For his heroic devotion to their cause
the people loved him with all the strength of their
hearts, and when he lost his life in their service they
lamented him as a saint and martyr.

Simon was born about the year 1208, at the Castle
of Montfort, in Normandy. His father had gained
great renown as a warrior, not free unfortunately
from the stain of cruelty. Under the title of the
Count of Toulouse, he had become one of the most
powerful nobles in France. He also bore the English
title of Earl of Leicester, and owned half the estates of
that English earldom. King John, however who was
on the English throne at that time, and who was
always ready to seize other men's goods, declared that
the earl had taken part in a conspiracy against him,
and in 1210 the Count was deprived of his English
estates. His increasing wealth and power in France
also brought him under the displeasure of the French
king and exposed him to the jealousy of the neighbouring nobles. The last years of his life were spent
in warfare against his enemies, and when he died most
of his possessions passed into the hands of the King
of France.

Upon his death, his eldest son, Amaury, claimed
the English lands which had belonged to his father.
King John had now been succeeded by Henry III,
who was disposed to be friendly to the De
Montfort family. He would not, however, allow
Amaury to hold lands in France and England at
the same time, and he bade him choose between
them. Amaury, who was a true Frenchman at
heart, would not give up his native lands, and he

therefore renounced his claim to the English estates in favour of his younger brother, Simon.

It was for the purpose of obtaining the title and estates of the earldom of Leicester that Simon de Montfort left his native country and settled among the people of whom he was one day to be the champion. He was received in a kindly way by Henry III., who gave him a generous pension and agreed to confer the earldom upon him.

SIMON AT THE ENGLISH COURT.

The young Earl of Leicester, as he now became, seems soon to have won the admiration of the king. He was handsome and strong, with a daring courage, a hot temper, and a strong will, which must have impressed a weak man like Henry. He must, indeed, have been singularly attractive in manner, for, in spite of his position, which was by no means important at this time, he gained the love of Eleanor, the king's sister. What is more remarkable still, he obtained the king's consent to their marriage. Henry gave the bride away himself, but the marriage was celebrated privately in the king's chapel, for Simon's friends feared that it would arouse much opposition in the country.

Princess Eleanor was a widow when Simon de Montfort won her love. She had been married when quite a child to William Marshall, Earl of Pembroke. When he died, his young widow was overwhelmed with grief, and, moved by the great love which she bore to her husband, she made a solemn vow, in the presence of the Archbishop of Canterbury and the Bishop of Gloucester, that she would never marry again. When, however, years passed by and her grief had become a thing of the past, the young princess thought no more of her early vow. When, therefore, Simon de Montfort, brave, handsome, and high-spirited, gained her love, she gave her consent to marry him.

Probably at the last moment the memory of her vow troubled her. Probably King Henry and Earl Simon feared the anger of the churchmen when they should hear the vow had been broken. These fears were well grounded, for no sooner did the news of the marriage become public than all parties in England—nobles, churchmen, and the people—expressed their indignation.

The nobles were angry because the king had not asked their advice in the matter. Henry, although married, was not yet a father, and the marriage of his sister was, therefore, an important matter to the English nation, because her children might become heirs to the throne. They were angry also because Simon de Montfort was a foreigner, and the nobles were already disgusted at the crowd of foreign favourites who surrounded the king, filling the high offices of the country and taking the king's affection from his English subjects.

The churchmen were horrified at the way in which Earl Simon's wife had broken her solemn vow. Edmund Rich, the Archbishop of Canterbury, denounced the unlawfulness of the marriage, and all the clergy and people were equally indignant.

The king's brother, Richard, Earl of Cornwall,

put himself at the head of the angry barons, and threatened Henry with civil war unless he dismissed his foreign favourites, and especially Simon, Earl of Leicester. The king found himself opposed by nearly all his barons, so that he was obliged to hold a conference, and to promise good government in future. He also made handsome presents to his brother Richard, in order to gain him over from the side of the barons. Earl Simon supported the king in this policy by entreaties and presents to Richard, until his heart was softened, and he yielded to his brother's promises of amendment. The barons, who had hoped for more vigorous measures, went away disappointed at the conduct of the Earl of Cornwall, and angry when they found that Simon de Montfort and he other foreign favourites still remained in power.

Earl Simon was probably at this time the most hated man in England. His countess was continually insulted by the people, who would not recognise her as Simon's lawful wife, so that she had to live in retirement in Kenilworth Castle, which the king had given her husband. Simon found his position unbearable, so that he decided to make a journey to Rome in order to induce the Pope to declare his marriage valid and legal. His journey was successful, and he returned to King Henry's Court on October 14th, 1240, having obtained the Pope's approval of his marriage. Shortly afterwards his eldest son was born at Kenilworth Castle. The king stood as the infant's godfather, and gave him the name of Henry.

ROYAL FAVOUR AND FICKLENESS.

The Earl of Leicester now enjoyed the highest favour of the king. Fresh honours, castles and lands were given to him, but the barons envied and hated him as the king's favourite. The following year the king's eldest son was born to the great rejoicing of the English people. They soon found, however, that they would have to pay dearly for their pleasure. The king sent out messengers to announce the happy event, and to receive rich gifts which he expected his people to make. Presents which he did not consider valuable enough he sent back with contempt until they were increased to his satisfaction. The people were astonished at the king's greed, and said to one another, "*God has given us this child, but the king sells him to us.*" Earl Simon was one of the godfathers of the royal infant, who was afterwards to become King Edward I. At this time the earl seemed the most fortunate man in England. He had married the king's sister; the nobles, clergy, and people no longer kept up their grievance against his marriage now that the Pope approved of it; and King Henry seemed to regard him with brotherly affection. It was not long, however, before an event happened which warned Earl Simon not to put his trust in princes, and showed him that royal favour is very often as fickle as an April day.

On the 9th of August, 1239, only a few weeks after he had stood as godfather to little Prince Edward, Earl Simon and his countess left their house to take part in a ceremony at court. **No**

THE QUARREL BETWEEN SIMON AND KING HENRY.

E

sooner did he appear than the king upbraided him before the whole court with violent words and reproaches. He accused him of vile crimes, and sternly commanded him to leave his presence. Simon was amazed at these passionate words, which were entirely unfounded. He withdrew from the court in dismay, and conducted his wife back again to Winchester House, on the Thames, where he was then living. No sooner, however, did they arrive than they were overtaken by messengers from the king with orders to drive them from their house. We are told that the earl departed blushing with anger, and as soon as the night fell he dropped down the Thames in a small vessel and set out for France with his wife and a few attendants.

There is no means of telling the cause of the king's anger, and we can only guess that he had believed the false accusations of Simon's enemies.

The earl took refuge with his relations in France, but it was not long before he was recalled to England by the fickle king. He returned, and was again received honourably by his royal brother-in-law, who tried to make amends for his former insults. But Simon only stayed in England long enough to collect sufficient money to enable him to go on a crusade to the Holy Land. History does not record his exploits in Palestine, but when he returned to England he found that the king was engaged in a war with France and earnestly desired his assistance. This war was a dreadful failure. Henry ventured into France without a proper army. He was unskilled in warfare, weak and hesitating, and it was owing entirely to the courage and devotion of Simon de Montfort that he was able to return to England with his liberty.

For the next five years Simon lived in peace and quiet at Kenilworth Castle. His countess had given him five sons, and he passed his days training them in all the exercises and accomplishments befitting young noblemen who might, in the future, play great parts in their country's history.

These peaceful days were interrupted by the king sending him to Gascony to put down a rebellion which had broken out there. This province in the south of France was the only French possession left in the hands of the English kings among all those which had belonged to Henry II. and his sons. Henry's government was as weak and unjust there as it was in England, and the Gascon nobles were continually rebelling against him.

Simon de Montfort no sooner trod the soil of Gascony than he set about restoring order with a strong will and an iron hand. The rebellious nobles soon found that a master had appeared among them. When they realised that it was useless to resist him, they sent over all sorts of base and false accusations against him to Henry. They accused him of needless cruelty, and of warring against them in order to become great and powerful himself. They also pretended that they were no longer rebelling against King Henry, but against the cruelty and injustice of Simon de Montfort.

Henry was weak and foolish enough to believe these false reports. He grew alarmed and angry with Earl Simon, and summoned him back to England to explain his conduct.

THE TRIAL OF EARL SIMON.

At Whitsuntide, in the year 1252, the Earl of Leicester was put upon his trial before the king and an assembly of barons. Simon had not only served the king well and faithfully in Gascony, but he had spent large sums of his own money in the king's service, so that he must have felt the deep injustice of being called upon to defend his conduct.

The trial lasted a whole month. One by one the earl answered the charges against him, quietly and clearly, so that everyone was satisfied except the suspicious king. Simon begged his royal brother - in - law to restore his confidence. He reminded him of his former services, and that he had promised to support him in Gascony for the six years during which the earl was to have been governor.

"Your words, my lord the king, should be kept sure and certain. Keep therefore the promise you made me; keep it according to the tenor of your charter, or pay me back the expenses I have incurred in your service." Thus spoke Earl Simon, but at these words the king burst into an ungovernable rage.

"Know this," he shouted, "I will keep none of my promises to an unworthy swindler and traitor like yourself. I may break my promise to one who breaks his, and behave coldly to one who clearly acts ill."

Earl Simon's haughty temper could not be restrained at this insult. With a fierce oath he swore that the king had lied. "Were you not shielded by the dignity of the royal name," he cried, 'it would be an ill hour for you in which you spoke such words. Do you call yourself a Christian? Do you believe yourself to be one? Have you ever confessed your sins?"

"Yes," shouted the king with a passion equal to the earl's.

"What avails confession," replied the earl bitterly, "without penance and satisfaction for your misdeeds?"

Beside himself with rage, the king answered, "I never repented of anything so much as I now repent of allowing you to enter England or to hold land and offices, so that you now wax fat and kick."

It would have gone ill with Earl Simon if the king had been able to wreak his vengeance upon him. Fortunately for him, however, the barons, who recognised the justice of his defence, protected him against the king's anger. Once more he was sent to Gascony, and once more he defeated the rebel Gascons, but his continual success only seemed to make the king listen more readily to the accusations and false reports of the earl's enemies.

EARL SIMON IN FRANCE.

In December, 1252, the Queen of France died, and the kingdom was left without a sovereign. It is a remarkable proof of the high reputation which Earl Simon must have gained that the French nobles besought him at this time to stay among them and become one of the guardians of thoroughly English in heart, and in spite of the insults and ingratitude he had received at the hands of the English king and of many of the barons, he refused this offer and would not desert his duties to England.

King Henry himself now set out for the rebellious province of Gascony, but in return for the Earl of Leicester's services he deposed him from his office of governor. The king, however, was never successful in war, and he was soon reduced to such straits by the turbulent Gascons that Simon de Montfort was able to revenge himself nobly by going to Henry's assistance. The king was only too glad of his help, and for a time the quarrel between the two men seemed to be patched up, although Simon at least could not easily forget the king's ill-treatment of him.

DISCONTENT IN ENGLAND.

For the next few years there was outward peace in England, but in the hearts of the people there was a growing discontent. The land was swarming with foreign adventurers brought over by the king. By flattery and cunning they induced the king to give them many of the most powerful castles and many of the richest estates in England, and they aroused the people's hatred by their arrogant behaviour. The king was always demanding money from the people, which went to enrich the hated foreigners or which was wasted upon inglorious or useless wars. In 1257 matters went from bad to worse. Owing to the failure of harvest, there was a dreadful famine, and the people were reduced to eat horseflesh and the bark of trees. In this year also the Welsh rebelled against the king, and more money was demanded from the unfortunate people for the expense of the war.

At Easter, in the year 1258, the king summoned his barons to a great council in order to grant him further sums of money and additional support against the Welsh.

Many of the barons were disgusted with the king's conduct. They determined to remonstrate against his misgovernment, and went to the great council full of this resolve.

It was Simon de Montfort, Earl of Leicester, who was the spokesman of their grievances. As soon as the barons had assembled, Earl Simon addressed them in eloquent language. He described the miserable condition of the country. He condemned the king for wasting large sums of money upon his foreign favourites. He said that he was so extravagant towards these foreigners that he had no money himself to spend upon the necessities of the country. He could not even defeat such an insignificant enemy as the Welsh. The earl ended this bold speech by urging the barons to take special measures against the king's misgovernment.

It is not difficult to imagine the king's anger at Earl Simon's vigorous reproaches, but he saw that the majority of the barons were on the earl's side. His brother Richard, the Earl of Cornwall, was abroad, and he was the only man powerful enough to curb the barons. Under these circumstances, Henry saw that he must submit, in appearance at least. He owned that he had been led astray by evil counsel, and swore solemnly to amend his ways. He consented that a number of barons should be appointed to meet at Oxford to draw up a plan of reform.

THE "PROVISIONS OF OXFORD."

Among those chosen for this purpose was the Earl of Leicester. He, indeed, was recognised by the barons as their leader. In the month of June, 1259, they assembled at Oxford with all their retainers fully armed. They were prepared to see that their plan of reform should be enforced, if need be, by a more powerful argument than words. The king saw that he was completely in their power, and he was obliged to give his consent to the plan of reform which they had prepared. This plan has become famous under the name of the " Provisions of Oxford."

By these " Provisions " the king undertook to do nothing without consulting a council of the barons. The chief officers of the kingdom were also to be appointed by this council, and every year they were to answer for their acts before the council and the king.

The barons next decided to get rid of the king's foreign favourites. They issued a decree that all the castles in the hands of these foreigners should be given up. Simon de Montfort was himself a foreigner by birth, and he therefore set the example by resigning his castles of Kenilworth and Odiham. The other foreigners refused, and were supported by Prince Edward, the king's eldest son. William de Valence, a foreigner who owned several castles in England, was among those who refused most violently to resign them. At last Earl Simon cut

his arguments short by crying fiercely, "The castles
or thy head!" The foreigners were terrified by this
threat. They knew also that if the nobles did not
carry out their intention, the whole mass of people
would besiege them and pull their castles about
their ears. Shortly afterwards they escaped secretly
from Oxford and went to Winchester. They were
pursued to this town by Earl Simon and his fellow-
barons, and at length the whole crowd of foreign
favourites fled in terror from England.

There was now universal rejoicing among the
people. Unbounded thanksgiving and praises were
heaped upon Simon de Montfort, whom the people
regarded as their champion and hero. His fame was
recorded in popular songs, and he was beloved by
every Englishman who had groaned under the
injustice and tyranny of King Henry.

DISSENSIONS AMONG THE BARONS.

For a time Simon de Montfort was the real head
of the country. The king was completely in his
power, and was obliged to agree to all his demands.
Gradually, however, the barons began to disagree
among themselves. Many of them began to think
that the king had been treated too harshly, and that,
after all, he was their king and ought to do pretty
much as he liked. Many of them also were jealous
of the power and popularity of Earl Simon. They
began to fear and dislike him for his haughty spirit
and hot temper. The earl was a strong-willed
determined man, and, like most people of that
character, he was impatient with anyone who balked
his purpose by timidity or half-measures. Now that

he had the king in his power, he determined to keep him so, and he did not hesitate to show his scorn for the barons who thought that the king might be given his liberty as he had promised to reform.

Robert de Clare, Earl of Gloucester, was the leader of the barons opposed to the Earl of Leicester. Earl Simon soon came to words with him. "I do not care," he said, "to live amongst men so changeable and so deceitful. We have made a common promise and taken a common oath to carry out these matters about which we are talking. You, my lord of Gloucester, are more bound to these wholesome statutes as being eminent above the rest."

At last the king and his son Edward escaped from Earl Simon's hands, and the kingdom was soon plunged in civil war. On the one side were the royal family and the barons who were jealous of the Earl of Leicester, and those who considered that the king ought not to be the slave of his people. On the other side were Earl Simon and his followers, who were determined that the king should keep the promises which he had made in the Provisions of Oxford for the exclusion of foreign favourites and the good government of the kingdom.

The royal army captured several of the most important towns in England, devastating the country in its progress. We are told by an old chronicler that "three comrades accompanied it—plunder, fire, and slaughter. There was no peace in the land; everything was destroyed by slaughter, fire, rapine, and robbery; everywhere was clamour and trembling and woe."

THE BATTLE OF LEWES.

At last Earl Simon and his fellow-barons came face to face with the royal army on the downs of Lewes, in Sussex. We are told that Earl Simon's army was inspired with a deep religious zeal. "So unanimous were they in their brotherly love that they did not fear to die for their country."

Before the battle, the Earl of Leicester dismounted from his horse, and addressed his soldiers in the following words:—

"Beloved comrades and followers, we are about to enter upon battle to-day in behalf of the government of the kingdoms. Let us pray to the King of all that, if what we now undertake pleases Him, He would grant us vigour and help, so that we may do a pleasing service, and overpower the malice of our enemies. Since we are His, to Him we commend our bodies and souls." Then all the soldiers fell upon the ground and stretched out their arms in the form of a cross, while they prayed, saying, "Grant us, O Lord, our desire of a glorious victory to the honour of Thy Name."

The right wing of Earl Simon's army was commanded by his two sons, Henry and Guy de Montfort. The earl himself was stationed with the reserve behind the main army, so that he and during his illness he had been carried about in this litter, so that when the enemy cast eyes upon it they would still believe that it contained the earl.

The battle began with a furious charge from Prince Edward, who attacked the Londoners in Earl Simon's army. It is said that, "like a hart desiring the waterbrooks, so thirsted he for the blood of the Londoners." The fury of his onslaught broke the ranks of the Londoners, and after a slight resistance they gave way and fled. Prince Edward pursued them for a great distance and slew great numbers. Upon his return, he attacked the men round Earl Simon's litter. His soldiers surrounded it with triumph. They thought that Earl Simon was now at their mercy.

"Come forth," they shouted. "Simon, thou devil! Come out of the litter, thou worst of traitors!"

But, as we know, the litter did not contain the earl. It was occupied by four traitors, bound hand and foot, who had tried to betray the City of London into the hands of the Royalists. It was only when Prince Edward's soldiers had destroyed the litter and its helpless occupants that they found they had been tricked.

Prince Edward, hot with exertion and rage, now returned to the battlefield, but it was too late. Many of the Royalists were already in full flight. The king's brother, Richard, had been made prisoner in a mill where he had taken refuge. The king himself was wounded, and had fled to the priory in the town of Lewes. The remnants of the army had taken refuge in Lewes Castle, which was being hotly besieged by Earl Simon's army.

Prince Edward managed to reach the castle,
at he saw that resistance was hopeless. The darkness of night was closing in when Earl Simon sent
proposals for a truce. They were accepted without delay, and the battle now ceased.

THE ENGLISH PARLIAMENT.

Once more King Henry and his son Edward
were in the power of the Earl of Leicester and the
victorious barons. Once more Earl Simon was the
real head and the ruling spirit of the country. It
is to be counted to his honour that he did not
desire this power for his personal glory, and he
used it only to protect the people from tyranny
and injustice. Indeed, he was wise enough to see
that, although it was necessary under the circumstances to keep guard over the king and his son,
yet it was a very disagreeable state of things, and
ought not to continue for long. Earl Simon was
in a very difficult position. He knew that he could
not always keep the king a prisoner, but he knew
also that directly he gave him his liberty he would
fall into all his old faults, and would waste the
people's money upon foreign favourites in the same
old way.

In Henry's time the government of the country
was carried on by the king and his ministers or
public officers. As the king appointed his ministers
himself, it was only natural that he should give
the great public offices to his favourites, and we
have seen that Henry chose foreigners, who treated
the people arrogantly and wasted their hard-earned
money.

The king and his ministers undertook the direction of the army, the building of cathedrals, churches, fortifications, and all the public works necessary for the prosperity and safety of the kingdom. To do all this a great deal of money, was needed, and when Norman kings first ruled over England they used to ask for as much money as they wanted. At first the kings were strong enough to force the people to give up their money whether they liked it or not, but by degrees they learnt that they could not always get what they wanted. We have read how Stephen Langton and the barons forced John to sign Magna Charta, and in this he promised to take only a *fair* amount of money from the barons and people for his own expenses or to use on public works. But it is not always easy to decide what is *fair*, and Magna Charta did not say who was to decide the question. If the king were strong, he took what he chose, and called it *fair*, and if he were weak the barons and citizens decided what was a *fair* amount to give him. We have seen that Henry III. wanted a great deal more money to spend upon himself and his favourites and the public expenses than the people considered fair.

Earl Simon was anxious to find a means by which he might give the king his liberty and at the same time protect the people's money. At last he devised a plan.

"Let the king," he said, "call together the barons and the citizens, and let him tell them how much money it is that he wants, and what he wants it for, and then it will be for the barons

THE BARONS ASKING HENRY III. TO SUMMON A PARLIAMENT.

and the people to say how much money they will give, and in what way it shall be collected. If the king asks what is right and just, then what he asks will be given to him, and it will be given all the more willingly because those who have to pay it will know for what purpose it is to be used, and will have given it of their own free will."

To carry out this plan, Earl Simon asked the king to call together a *Parliament* to help him to govern the country. As the king was still completely in the earl's power, he could not refuse his request, and in a short time a number of the principal men of the country were summoned to form the Parliament.

First of all came the barons, but only twenty-three of them, for many were jealous of Earl Simon or afraid of offending the king. Next came one hundred and twenty churchmen, and, lastly, from every county a certain number of members were chosen, called "Knights of the Shire," and from every large town a "burgess."

The barons and churchmen who sat in this first Parliament represent the temporal and spiritual leers who sit in the House of Lords of our modern Parliament. The "Knights of the Shire" and the "burgesses" represent the members of Parliament who sit in our House of Commons. Indeed, even at the present day the Members of Parliament who are chosen by the counties are sometimes called "Knights of the Shire," and those who are elected by the towns are called "Borough Members," which is a similar expression to "burgess."

Earl Simon did not invent an entirely new

scheme when he asked the king to summon a Parliament. English kings had often summoned barons and clergy to a "Great Council" to advise them how to govern the country. Four times before, indeed, "Knights of the Shire" had been summoned to the Great Council. Never before, however, had the *towns* sent members to the Council, and for this reason Simon de Montfort has the honour of having formed the first real Parliament. He was the first to see that all classes in the country must be represented in order to make a complete Parliament. He was the first to see that the towns, which contained the most important and wisest citizens of England, should have a share in the government of the country. Many centuries had to pass before Parliament obtained the influence and power which it now possesses, but it was Simon de Montfort who gave it its life and who recognised its importance. For this great service to his country he is deserving of all praise and honour.

The first English Parliament lasted from January 20th to the middle of March of the year 1265. Peace was once more established in the land, and the king promised to rule according to the old English liberties and rights laid down in Magna Charta and elsewhere.

EARL SIMON'S ENEMIES.

For a time all went well, but by degrees the old jealousy against Simon de Montfort broke out once more among the barons. They accused him of grasping at power for his own ambition and advancement. Everything that he did, everything that he said, was criticised with a bitter spirit of envy and hatred. Complaints were made against his sons, who, by this time, had reached man's estate. Unfortunately for himself, Earl Simon was not a man to keep a friend or to win over an enemy by soft words. He hated hypocrisy and loved plain-speaking. He did not hesitate to denounce his enemies in scornful terms, and his temper was always ready to blaze out at any insult or ill-doing.

Earl Simon's old enemy, Richard, **Earl of** Gloucester, was now dead, but his young son Gilbert, who had at first been friendly to the earl's cause, deserted him and became his open enemy. He was soon joined by a number of other barons, who were all eager to wreak their spite against the man who had defended them against the king's tyranny.

Prince Edward escaped from the guardianship of Earl Simon, and joined the Earl of Gloucester and his barons. Civil **war** once more broke out, and soon the brave old Earl of Leicester saw himself deserted, one by one, by a large number of his former adherents.

On June 28th, 1265, he summoned his younger son Simon to his aid. Young Simon de Montfort was in the west of England with a small force of soldiers, with whom **he** was guarding the peace in the counties of Dorset, Devonshire, and Somerset. When he received his father's message, he proceeded in a very leisurely way to obey the summons. At Kenilworth he stopped for a while, neglecting to place his soldiers within the walls of the castle to guard against a sudden attack from the enemy. A

F

woman spy carried the news of his carelessness to the Royalist forces commanded by Prince Edward, and these suddenly surrounded Kenilworth and attacked young de Montfort's force. They were taken completely by surprise, most of them were killed, but young Simon managed to escape from his enemies, and took refuge in the castle. Prince Edward did not stay to attack the castle, but marched rapidly towards Earl Simon, hoping to take him by surprise.

THE BATTLE OF EVESHAM.

The earl was stationed at Evesham. He was anxiously awaiting the approach of his son, for he had not heard of his disaster. The king was still in the earl's power, and Simon was supported by a small army of barons and their retainers who remained faithful to his cause.

On the morning of Tuesday, August 4th, the king heard mass in the abbey, and then breakfasted, but the earl would take nothing. As soon as the king had finished breakfast, the earl and his troops prepared to mount their horses in order to proceed to Kenilworth. At this moment, however, some scouts ran in to say that an armed troop was approaching.

At this message the earl cried out joyfully, "It is my son." Then, to make sure, he added, "Go up and look, and bring me word again." His barber, Nicholas, was gifted with long sight and had a knowledge of heraldry, and the earl mounted with this man to the bell-tower of the abbey. At first Nicholas distinguished the banners of young

Simon de Montfort fluttering in the breeze, but the next moment he saw that they were carried in the hands of enemies, and that behind them floated the royal standards. When Earl Simon heard the words of his barber, he knew that his fate was sealed. He looked out of the bell-tower, and saw the gleaming arms of his enemies approaching the town. Behind him lay the river Avon, spanned by a bridge, which was the only means of escape. Even this last chance was barred, for as he looked he saw a troop of horsemen dashing from the opposite direction to guard the bridge. To the right Earl Simon's eyes followed the course of the Avon and looked towards Kenilworth, where he had spent the most peaceful years of his life with his wife and children. Down below the golden corn was ripening in the sun, and the little town of Evesham was surrounded by fair gardens. This peaceful scene was soon to be disturbed by the horrid sounds of war, and the blooming flowers would soon be stained with blood. Earl Simon turned away from the bell tower with a sigh. "May the Lord have mercy on our souls," he said, "for our bodies are undone."

Their forces were outnumbered by three to one, and it was useless to hope for victory. The earl's friends tried to persuade him to fly, but he disdained to do so. In his turn, he urged his sons and comrades to save themselves, but one and all they refused to desert him, saying that they desired not to live if their leader died.

"Come then," he said, "and let us die like men, for we have fasted here, and we shall break fast in heaven."

When he saw Prince Edward's troops advancing with perfect discipline, the thought of his approaching death did not check a burst of admiration, and he was proud to think that they had learnt their knowledge of warfare from himself. "By the arm of St. James," he cried, "they come on well; they learnt that, not from themselves, but from me."

The battle began with a furious onslaught from Prince Edward's troops. It soon developed into a massacre, and the flower gardens ran red with the blood of the earl's followers. Earl Simon's horse was killed under him, and then he learnt that his eldest son Henry was dead. When he heard the news, he cried, "Is it so? Then, indeed, it is time for me to die." With these words he rushed upon his enemy with increased fury, and laid about him with his sword with such fearful force that a witness of the fight stated that if there had been but six more like himself the tide of battle would have been turned. At length a soldier lifted up the earl's coat of mail and struck him in the back. With the words "Dieu merci!" upon his lips, the old warrior fell and died.

For two hours longer the battle raged, until Earl Simon's followers were strewn round their leader in dead and dying heaps. Thus the battle ended, and the Royalists were triumphant. Even now they would not leave Earl Simon in the peace of death, but they treated his body with horrid brutality.

Nevertheless, although the Royalists could destroy Earl Simon's body, they could not destroy the love which lived in the hearts of the English citizens for their brave protector. They cherished his memory as a martyr and saint, and there are quaint old songs which still survive and show how the people regarded him as their champion and hero.

In private life Simon de Montfort was an example to all Englishmen. He was a good husband, a loving father, a faithful friend, and in all things the model of a Christian gentleman.

The good work which he did during his life lived after his death. The prince who had defeated him at the battle of Evesham learnt, in after life, to admire the noble qualities of his old enemy. When he became Edward I., he followed his good example in many ways, and especially in governing the kingdom with the advice and consent of a Great Council similar to that First Parliament formed by Simon de Montfort.

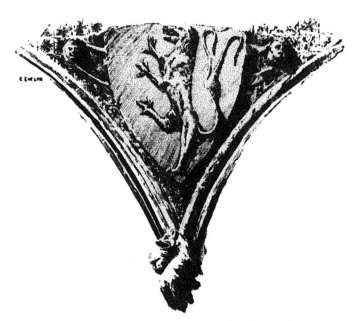

THE ARMS OF SIMON DE MONTFORT.

MICROCOPY RESOLUTION TEST CHART

(ANSI and ISO TEST CHART No. 2)

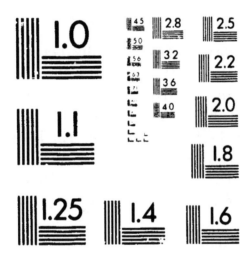

APPLIED IMAGE Inc

. . . . .st Main Street
. . . . . New York   14609   USA
. . . . : . 00 – Phone
. . . . . 989 – Fax

IV.

SIR FRANCIS DRAKE

AND

THE NEW WORLD.

IN the "golden days" of Queen Elizabeth the county of Devon was the birthplace of some of the most famous heroes in English history. John Hawkins, the patriarch of English seamen; Martin Frobisher and Humphrey Gilbert, the first Englishmen who sailed far into the Arctic regions; Walter Raleigh, Queen Elizabeth's brilliant courtier; Richard Grenville, the hero of the good ship *Revenge*, which kept at bay fifty Spanish men-of-war—all these, and many other brave Englishmen, were born and bred on the rugged coast of Devon.

In the year 1540 another great Englishman was born in this same county of Devon. This was Francis Drake, who was destined to surpass the fame of his Devonshire comrades and to carry the English flag into seas which no English ship had ever sailed before.

At an early age his parents removed from his birthplace at Tavistock, to Chatham, where his father had been appointed a naval chaplain. It was here, in the busy dockyard which resounded day after day with the building of ships and the loading and un-loading of merchant vessels, that Francis Drake learnt to love ships and shipping and to long for a

SIR FRANCIS DRAKE.

(*From the Statue by Sir J. E. Boehm, R.A., on Plymouth Hoe.*)

life of adventure. As he played about the dockyards
and watched the bronzed sailors coiling their ropes
or repainting their vessels, he heard many a strange
story of foreign lands which made his heart beat with
excitement. In those days of King Henry VIII. and
Queen Elizabeth, the world was very different from
these times, when railways cross every continent
and floating palaces steam rapidly over the oceans
from one half of the globe to the other. Nowadays
every schoolboy knows the shape of the world, and, if
he has a map before him, he can readily point out
America and Australia and tell a good deal about
them.

"THE NEW WORLD."

When Francis Drake was a boy playing about
Chatham Dockyard, things were very different. A large
part of the world was, as it were, hidden by a cloud,
with only here and there a glimpse of light breaking
through the darkness. The great continent of
Australia had never been seen by Europeans, only
the northern parts of Africa were known, and no
English vessel had ever entered the Pacific Ocean.
A century had not yet passed since Christopher
Columbus had sailed from Spain across the Atlantic
and discovered that a great country existed—a " New
World," as he called it—which until then had been
utterly unknown to Europeans.

Soon after this great discovery other vessels
followed in the track of Columbus across the western
sea, and the " New World," or America, as it is now
called, was gradually explored.

It is to the Spaniards and Portuguese that the
honour of these first discoveries is due. Two daring

Spaniards, Lizano and Cortes, explored Mexico and Peru, and brought back to Spain specimens of the gold, silver, and precious stones with which the soil was richly stocked. These riches inflamed the cupidity of the Spanish nation. Hundreds of daring Spaniards sailed across the Atlantic to obtain some of the wealth in the gold and silver mines of Mexico, Brazil, and Peru, or to bring back spices and pearls from the West India Islands. The Spaniards soon founded thriving colonies, and their courage and daring gradually built up a Spanish Empire in the " New World," so that the King of Spain became the richest and most powerful sovereign in Europe. The Spaniards, however, always took care not to tell the secret of the world's geography to other nations. They were anxious to prevent sailors of other countries from following the Spanish vessels across the Atlantic, lest they should seize some of the riches which Spain was greedy to keep entirely to herself.

Shortly, however, before the birth of Francis Drake, Englishmen began to ask one another what right had Spain to claim the known and unknown countries which lay beyond the Atlantic. Marvellous stories reached their ears of the vast wealth which the Spaniards were bringing back from their new colonies. English ships began to venture across the ocean to find out a means of obtaining a share of these riches. In those days ships were small—most of them, indeed, no larger than a gentleman's yacht of the present day—and many dangers and difficulties had to be overcome before they could reach the " New World." But English sailors did not lack for courage, and now and again an English vessel ploughed its way across the Atlantic and returned, laden with spices bought from Spanish merchants, while the sailors were full of the wonders which they had seen and heard.

These stories, as they passed from mouth to mouth, became exaggerated in the telling. Francis Drake, listening to the yarns of the weather-beaten sailors at Chatham, heard many a story as marvellous as that of Othello in Shakespeare's play, when he discoursed :

> "Of moving accidents by flood and field ;
> Of hair-breadth 'scapes i' the imminent deadly breach ;
> Of being taken by the insolent foe,
> And sold to slavery . . . . .
> And of the Cannibals that each other eat,
> The Anthropophagi, and men whose heads
> Do grow beneath their shoulders."

It was not long before Englishmen began to envy the wealth of Spain, and were eager to share it with her. This envy gradually changed into a fierce hatred. At this time a deadly struggle was proceeding throughout Europe between Catholics and Protestants. The Spaniards had retained the Roman Catholic faith, while the English had become Protestants. Unfortunately both parties forgot those Christian commands which order us to love one another, to forgive our enemies, and to live in peace and charity. A terrible religious war took place which bathed Christian countries in blood. Great crimes were committed on both sides. Protestants were burnt, tortured, and murdered by Catholics, and, in return, Catholics were tortured and killed by Protestants. Spain was the most powerful country which still held the Catholic faith, and it was therefore hated more fiercely than any other by Protestant nations. Outwardly, England was at peace with Spain, but in the hearts of the English people a hatred was gradually growing up against the name of Spaniard which threatened to break out into open warfare.

Every year vessels came into Chatham bringing stories of English sailors seized in Spanish ports, cast into Spanish dungeons, or burnt in the market-places. Then came other vessels, and English sailors rubbed their hands with glee when they told how they had robbed Spanish vessels of rich stores of gold and precious stones and cast the Spanish sailors overboard. sewn up in the sails of their own ships.

These were the stories which filled the ears of young Francis Drake as he watched the vessels in Chatham Dockyard. There can be no surprise that two resolutions should have taken root in his heart: first, a resolve to sail out into the west to discover new lands and bring back riches, and, secondly, a fierce and bitter hatred of Spain, with a determination to revenge the cruelties which Spaniards were practising upon Englishmen.

DRAKE'S EARLY DAYS.

Francis Drake soon learnt something about foreign lands. At an early age he was apprenticed to the skipper of a small merchant vessel which traded between France and Holland. On this stout little ship Drake learnt to brave the dangers of the sea, and the rough winds which blew down the Channel hardened his body and spirit into sturdy manhood. His courage and honesty, the brightness of his blue

eyes, the frankness of his ruddy, handsome face, won
him the love of his skipper, and when the old fellow
died he left his vessel to the Devonshire lad who had
been his faithful lieutenant.   Drake was now his
own master, and he determined to carry out the
hopes of his boyhood.   The King of Spain had for-

CITIZENS IN THE DAYS OF DRAKE.

bidden his subjects in the West Indies to carry on
trade with foreigners; but Drake snapped his fingers
at King Philip, and resolved to set this command
at naught.
    One fine day he sailed out of Plymouth harbour
into the Western Ocean. For the first time he now
set eyes on the "New World," and although he saw
none of the fabled monsters which had filled his

boyish imagination, he yet saw enough wonders to
make him eager for more. For some time he traded
with the Spaniards. They quietly ignored the command of their king, and were quite willing to sell
their goods to anyone who had money to buy them.
One day, however, Francis Drake found himself in
an awkward corner. He was surrounded by Spanish
men-of-war who had been sent out specially to stop
his traffic with the colonists, and, in order to escape
with his life and liberty, Master Drake was obliged
to give up his cargo. The hot-tempered Devonshire seaman returned to England uttering many
vows of vengeance against Spain which he never
forgot

Queen Elizabeth was now on the throne of England. This great queen was fortunate enough to be
surrounded by wise counsellors and brave soldiers
and sailors who were eager to make England the
most prosperous and the most powerful nation in
the world. They saw well enough that Spain was
rapidly becoming so great and wealthy that unless
her progress were checked she would become the
mistress of the world. Queen "Bess" and her
counsellors looked about for a plan to arrest the
power of Spain, and for men who would carry out
the plan.

In those days the English navy consisted of only
a few royal ships. In time of war these ships were
supported by armed merchant vessels, and, in peace,
it was by no means rare for the queen to employ
the royal ships in commercial enterprises. It sometimes happened that when these armed vessels found
themselves alongside a foreign vessel loaded with

stores, they did not hesitate to proclaim the law of
might as against *right*, and they took by force the
cargo of their foreign neighbour. In time of war this
practice was openly encouraged by the sovereigns of
the conflicting countries, but it was supposed to be
forbidden in time of peace.

Queen Elizabeth did not wish to go to war openly
with Spain, but she did not look with displeasure
upon any English seaman who might be bold enough
to capture a Spanish treasure ship. If King Philip
of Spain sent her angry remonstrances against the
bold deeds of her seamen, she replied that they were
done without her knowledge and consent, and that
she was "very sorry." The crafty queen knew that
Spain desired peace rather than war, and she secretly
encouraged her seamen to lay hands on Spanish
merchant vessels.

Queen "Bess" soon came to hear that a young
Devonshire sailor, named Francis Drake, was a man
of wonderful courage and daring, who was eager to
sail out to the West Indies to revenge himself upon
the Spaniards. There were many people who were
ready to put their trust in Francis Drake, and they
supplied him with money in order that he might
equip an expedition against the Spaniards. The
Spaniards complained afterwards that the queen herself had given Drake money for this purpose.
Whether this be true or not is uncertain, but it is
a fact that when Drake sailed out of Plymouth Sound
on Whitsunday eve, 1572, he was in command of
two little vessels fitted out in every way like her
Majesty's own men-of-war. Francis Drake himself
was on board the *Pasha*, and his brother John was

in command of the *Swan*. The crews of both ships together numbered but seventy-three men and boys, and amongst these only one had reached the age of thirty. With this tiny force at his command, Drake resolved to carry out a plan so daring that it seemed more like an adventure of one of King Arthur's knights than the work of an English seaman. This plan was nothing less than to seize the Spanish port of Nombre di Dios in South America, and to empty into the holds of his own vessels some of the wealth stored up in the treasure-house of the world.

IN THE GOLDEN WEST.

Out into the west sailed the two little vessels, and after many days they anchored in a secluded bay on the coast of South America. Here Drake intended to fit up three light boats which he had brought in pieces from Plymouth. Very soon a clearing was made in the luxuriant vegetation which grew to the very edge of the sea-shore, and here the carpenters got busily to work upon the boats. They were interrupted by seeing three vessels sailing towards the little harbour. Instantly the alarm was given. Drake ordered his comrades to arm themselves, for he knew that if the vessels were Spanish he and his seamen would soon have to fight for their lives. Fortunately it turned out to be an English vessel commanded by Captain James Rause, with two Spanish ships which he had captured. When the newcomers learnt the object of Drake's expedition, they eagerly requested to join him, and an agreement was thereupon written down and signed by the two commanders.

In a week the three pinnaces were ready, and the little fleet sailed out of the bay. They crept along the coast to the Isthmus of Panama until, after five days, they reached a group of islands which they knew by the name of Prisoners' Islands. Here they landed, and Drake encouraged his men by a cheering speech. Then he picked out fifty-three of the bravest and most trustworthy fellows, and, leaving the vessels in charge of Captain Rause, he put his men into four boats and rowed swiftly towards the bay of Nombre di Dios.

At midnight they reached the entrance to the bay. All night long they rested on their oars, waiting with beating hearts for the approach of dawn. Before them lay, in deathlike silence, the town of Nombre di Dios, where vast quantities of gold, silver and precious stones were stored up in the Spanish treasure-houses. Not a light was to be seen. Not a roof or spire appeared through the darkness, but Drake and his comrades knew that Spanish guns were facing them, ready to blow them out of the water at the first alarm. Presently the sky was streaked with silver light. The moon was breaking through a cloud, but Drake declared it to be the approach of dawn. He ordered his men to row towards the town, but, at the same moment, they perceived the dark shadow of a boat leave the side of a ship in the harbour and dart towards the town. With a shout he urged his men forward, and the boats dashed through the water after the Spaniards. The latter saw that they were being overtaken, and, turning the prow of their boat, they fled to the opposite side of the bay.

Now Drake and his men ran their boat alongside
the quay, and tumbled the Spanish guns into the sand.
In a few minutes the whole town had taken alarm.
At first, the shouts of men, and women's shrieks,
met their ears. Then the roll of a drum thundered
out with a continuous din, calling the citizens to
arms, and finally the church bell swung backwards
and forwards, pealing above the tumult.

Drake dashed into the centre of the town,
followed by his men. Here they were received by
a volley of musketry from a body of Spanish
soldiers. Drake's trumpeter fell dead, and several
of his men were badly wounded, but they dashed
upon the Spaniards with sword and pike and hearty
English shouts. The Spaniards were bewildered
in the darkness, and their imagination multiplied
the number of their foes. They made a stout
resistance, but the fierce onslaught of the English
seamen beat them back until they threw down
their arms and fled in tumult towards the gates of
the town.

Drake now marched to one of the Government
storehouses and broke into it with a few of his men
while the others guarded the market place. As they
entered, a marvellous sight met their eyes. Piled high
against the walls stood solid bars of silver of enormous
length and thickness. The English seamen gaped with
wonder at the sight of all this wealth glittering in
the moonlight. They prepared to seize some of the
silver, but Drake forbade them to touch it. He
knew that there was another treasure-house in the
town stocked full of gold and precious stones, worth
a hundred times more than the silver. By his

G

orders they left the storehouse and joined their comrades in the market place.

By this time a crowd of citizens was pouring into the market place to defend their town from the sudden invasion. The drums were beating, the bell still rocked to and fro, and, to add to the wild tumult, a terrific storm burst and a deluge of rain poured down. Drake's men began to get nervous, and their captain had hard work to keep them steady. He tried to rally them by cheery words, and when that failed, by taunts.

" I have brought you," he cried, " to the mouth of the treasure-house of the world. Blame nobody but yourselves if you go away empty."

Upon these words he stepped forward with a hearty shout, but in another moment he uttered a groan and rolled over in the sand. It appeared that he had received a horrible wound in the leg during his first dash upon the town, but he had concealed it from his men so that it might not dispirit them. Now he had fallen, faint with loss of blood, and he seemed in a dangerous condition. Even now, however, he gasped out entreaties to his men to stand firm, but they would not listen to his words.

" Your life," they cried, " is dearer to us than all the wealth of the Indies."

Carefully and tenderly they carried him back to the boats, and as the sun rose and showed the Spaniards what a handful of men had stormed their town, the four boats rowed out of the harbour, and the King of Spain's treasures remained untouched.

After this disappointment Drake sailed farther

along the coast. His wound soon healed, and then he landed to explore the surrounding country. He also wanted to obtain information about the route by which the Spanish treasure from the mines of Peru was carried to the coast in order to be shipped to Spain.

In the woods they came upon a party of runaway slaves called Cimaroons. These savages carried on a deadly warfare against the Spaniards, who had formerly been their masters. When they heard that Drake and his party were also enemies of the Spaniards they readily agreed to join them and to guide them to a place where they could surprise a caravan of treasure-laden mules passing on their way to the coast. They led Drake through the forest to a watershed from which the streams flow on one side to the Atlantic and on the other side to the Pacific. As the thick undergrowth obscured the view, Drake mounted to the top of a tall tree. From this height he saw, stretched before his eyes, for the first time, the glittering waves of the Pacific Ocean. As the magnificent sight burst upon his view Drake was filled with enthusiasm and longing, and we are told that "he besought Almighty God of His goodness to grant him life and leave to sail once in an English ship in that sea."

After many exciting adventures the English seamen were conducted by the Cimaroons to a narrow pass through which the treasure - laden mules were driven from Panama. Drake placed his men in hiding on each side of the pass. They had not long to wait. In a short time they heard the tinkling of the mule bells as they approached.

Presently some Spanish soldiers cantered past unconscious of the men lying each side of them in the long grass. Still the mule train came on, carelessly and leisurely, with bells jingling, and an occasional crack of a whip or a shout from one of the drivers. Then, suddenly, a shrill whistle was blown. It was a signal from Drake, and at the same moment the English seamen sprang from the grass and with shouts of triumph dashed upon the soldiers and drivers surrounding the train of mules. The Spaniards were taken completely by surprise, and after discharging their muskets at Drake and his comrades, with no effect, they fled in terror down the road.

Not a moment was lost by the English seamen. With their long knives they slashed open the packages on the mules, and loaded themselves with gold, pearls, rubies, emeralds, and diamonds. Then they buried fifteen tons of silver which was too heavy for them to carry. Staggering under their burden of treasures they made their way back to their ships, and were well out of danger by the time the Spaniards had recovered from their panic and returned.

After many other adventures Drake turned the prows of his vessels homewards. He arrived in England on Sunday, August 9th, 1573. The good people of Plymouth were listening to their Sunday morning sermon when Drake arrived in port. We are told that "the news of his return did so speedily pass over all the church, and surpass their minds with desire and delight to see him, that very few, or none, remained with the preacher, all hastening to see the evidence of God's love and blessing towards our gracious queen and country."

When the news of Drake's exploits gradually leaked out, everyone in England was not so well pleased as the good folks of Plymouth. Several statesmen of Queen Elizabeth told their mistress that Drake was nothing more than a pirate who had stolen other people's goods, and who ought to be hanged. But Queen " Bess " did not look upon Drake's adventures in this light. It was true that England was not openly at war with Spain, but everyone knew that the King of Spain was only waiting for a convenient opportunity to declare war. In the meantime Spanish sailors were seizing English vessels in their ports, burning English sailors in their market-places, and doing everything in their power to ruin English trade. Considering these facts, the Queen, who dearly loved a brave man and a daring deed, was not inclined to blame Francis Drake for giving the Spaniards tit-for-tat. England was not yet ready for war, and the officers of Spain were too much on the alert to allow crafty Queen " Bess " to openly reward Drake for his services, but she did not hesitate to give him secret help and encouragement.

DRAKE'S VOYAGE ROUND THE WORLD.

Four years later, on November 15th, 1577, Francis Drake again sailed out of Plymouth Sound bound for the Spanish Indies. The vessels which he commanded were not much larger than a modern fishing smack, and the crews amounted, all told, to only 160 men and boys. Drake himself sailed on board the *Pelican*, and behind him came a fleet of small vessels consisting of the *Elizabeth*, the *Christopher*, the *Marigold*, and the *Swan*.

The Spanish Ambassador in London heard of this new expedition. He learnt, too, that it was commanded by the man whom every Spaniard had learnt to fear by the name of *El Draque*, the dragon. King Philip of Spain immediately sent out orders to his colonists in the West Indies to sink every English ship and to hang every English sailor that appeared in the Caribbean Sea. It seemed impossible that any English ship should ever find its way to the Pacific Ocean, so that no warning was sent to the Spaniards in that part of the world. The Spaniards had not fully learnt the daring and determination of *El Draque*, but they were soon to be taught a painful lesson.

At first the expedition did not progress favourably. Terrible weather set in, and the vessels were sorely beaten about. Worse than this, Drake was constantly annoyed and alarmed by the treacherous actions of a gentleman on board one of the ships, who tried to create a mutiny among the seamen. This personage was Thomas Doughty, a man of good birth and education, who had formerly been a secretary of Sir Walter Raleigh. He had been one of Drake's most intimate friends, but in this expedition he seemed insanely jealous of Drake's position, and did his utmost to ruin his plans.

By degrees the weather mended, and Drake's vessels sped before the wind across the Bay of Biscay, past the Cape de Verde Islands, and then **right over the Atlantic until they touched the**

South American Continent, and entered the mouth
of the River Plate. Their fortune now prospered,
but one day Drake lost sight of the small vessel
commanded by Thomas Doughty. Drake had already
lost faith in his former friend, and he sent the
Marigold in chase of the missing vessel. Doughty's
ship was quickly overtaken, and in order to prevent
the traitor from playing false again, Drake burnt
the ship, distributed the crew among the other
vessels, and put Doughty on his own ship. Then
they sailed on until they came to Port St. Julian
on the coast of Patagonia.

As they entered the deserted harbour a grue-
some object met their eyes. A skeleton, with bones
picked clean by vultures, was swinging to and fro
on a gallows-tree. It was the skeleton of a man
who had been executed for mutiny fifty years before
by the Portuguese explorer, Magellan.

This dreadful spectacle reminded Drake that he
also had a man on board who deserved death for
his treachery. Thomas Doughty had never ceased
uttering complaints against Drake, and urging his
men to mutiny against their commander. Drake
knew well that his expedition could never succeed
without the strictest discipline, and he resolved to
make an example of his former friend. Doughty was
brought before a court-martial composed of the officers
of the expedition, and placed upon his trial according
to the customs of English law. The facts were not
difficult to prove, and he was found guilty of treason.
Then Drake demanded that he should be punished
according to the gravity of his crime.

"They that think this man worthy of death,'

he cried, "let them, with me, hold up their hands."

The words were scarcely out of his lips before he was surrounded by a number of sunburnt hands, and Doughty was condemned to die.

On a small island near the coast, a tragic scene now took place which struck awe into the hearts of the English sailors. Tables were spread with the best stores in the ships, and hard by were placed an altar and a block side by side. The two men who had formerly been friends knelt at the altar and prayed together. Then the seamen seated themselves at the tables with Doughty in their midst, and drank to the man who was about to leave them on his last journey. Doughty faced his death with great courage, and before kneeling at the block he embraced Drake affectionately. He recognised his guilt, and acknowledged the justice of his punishment. Then the sword fell, and Drake, calm and unmoved, cried out: "Lo, this is the end of traitors!"

After this tragic execution Drake and his mariners remained six weeks at Port St. Julian, sheltering themselves in the bay against the stormy weather which raged during that time. Drake burnt one of his vessels which was too small to face the weather of those seas, and now only three ships remained—the *Pelican*, the *Elizabeth*, and the *Marigold*. At last his patience would hold out no longer, and in spite of the bad weather he sailed out of Port St. Julian to the Strait of Magellan.

This strait forms a long and dangerous passage

through the southern part of South America. In those days it was believed that this was the only way from the Atlantic into the Pacific, for it was supposed that the continent of America extended without break as far as the South Pole.

Francis Drake had no charts, and he sent his small boats on ahead of the ships to take soundings of the depth of the water. It was a perilous undertaking. At any moment the ships might strike on a rock or ground in shallow water. On either side of them snow-covered mountains overhung the strait, and a heavy snowstorm obscured the view. So difficult was the task that Drake was three weeks in getting his vessels through the narrow passage, which was seventy miles long.

At last they entered the Pacific—that marvellous ocean into which Drake had once prayed that he might sail with an English ship. Now he hoped that the greatest difficulties had been conquered, but he was doomed to disappointment. As they left the Strait of Magellan they were met by the most terrific storm that they had ever experienced. The sturdy English vessels trembled and quaked before the fury of the tempest, so that Drake and his mariners almost gave themselves up as lost. They were beaten back by a roaring westerly gale six hundred miles to the south-east of Cape Horn, which is the southernmost point of South America.

By this misfortune Drake learnt a great lesson in geography. The wind which had tossed him so far out of his course, taught him that the Strait of Magellan was not the only passage from the Atlantic to the South Pole as men had formerly believed.

This lesson was learnt at a heavy cost. Round Cape Horn a gale blows continually, and the waves are always higher than in any other part of the world. In this tumult of wind and water the stout little vessel, the *Marigold*, went down, and every man on board perished with her. Then Captain Wynter, who was in command of the *Elizabeth*, made his way back to the Strait of Magellan; but after waiting there three weeks, instead of going to Valparaiso, where he had agreed to meet Drake if they were separated, he lost heart and turned the prow of his vessel homewards, much against the will of his mariners.

Drake was now alone on his vessel, whose name he changed from the *Pelican* to the *Golden Hind*. He anchored among some islands where the waters of the Pacific and the Atlantic meet in a rough embrace. No Englishman, and perhaps no white man, had ever set foot in this region. Drake was filled with gladness at the thought, and one day he landed on the furthest island, and walking alone to the end, he laid himself down and embraced the southernmost point of the known world.

Drake now sailed to Valparaiso, hoping to find Captain Wynter waiting for him in the harbour. But Wynter was on his way to England, and Drake found instead a great Spanish merchant vessel, the *Grand Captain of the South*, lying lazily at anchor until the wind should rise and carry her to Panama with her cargo of gold and Chili wine. The Spanish sailors hanging over the bulwarks of their vessel espied Drake's sail approaching the harbour, and, never dreaming of an English ship, they brought up

a cask of wine to give a merry welcome to the newcomers. A boat left the side of Drake's ship and
rowed alongside the Spanish galleon. The Spaniards
beat a welcome with their drum, but suddenly they
fell back with dismay. A dozen English sailors
sprang on board and laid about them with their
fists. A desperate scuffle took place. but before the
astonished Spaniards could seize their weapons, they
were made prisoners and locked under the hatches
of their own ship. Then Drake and his mariners
quickly conveyed the gold and wine on to their own
ship. For three days the *Golden Hind* lay in the
harbour, while the English mariners collected provisions from the little colony of Spaniards at
Valparaiso.

With a very good stock of fresh victuals they
now set sail for Tarapaca, where silver from the
Andes mines was put on board ship to be conveyed
to Panama. Here again the Spaniards never dreamt
of being disturbed by an Englishman. On the quays
the silver bars were piled up ready for loading, and
the muleteers who had brought them to the coast
were sleeping in the sunshine a few yards off. Drake
and his men did not disturb the Spaniards from their
slumbers, but they quietly took possession of the
silver. As soon as they had begun to carry it to
their ship another train of mules entered the town,
laden with a similar treasure. The drivers were too
surprised to resist the demand of the English sailors,
and in a short while the *Golden Hind* sailed away
with her rich cargo

At the town of Lima, Drake found the harbour
full of shipping, and he amused himself and terrified

the Spaniards at the same time by going from ship
to ship in search of gold. Not a grain did he
find, and after his vessel had been lying in the
harbour for two days, the Viceroy of Peru marched
down to the coast with a thousand soldiers, and sent
out four vessels to capture Drake dead or alive. But
the Spaniards did not like to tackle such a dangerous
enemy as *El Draque*, as they called him, and Drake
sailed away without so much as a pistol-shot being
sent after him.

Now he captured ship after ship as he sailed
along, and emptied them all of anything that he
needed for his own use. From one of these prizes
he learnt that an enormous Spanish galleon was
sailing in those waters laden with a vast treasure
bound for Panama. Drake heard the news with glee,
and there and then resolved that Panama should
never set eyes on an ounce of these riches. He
promised a golden chain to the first man who should
catch sight of the galleon. Away went the *Golden
Hind* with every inch of canvas set, racing before
the wind towards Panama. At last, off Cape San
Francisco, Drake's young nephew, John, espied the
treasure-laden galleon ploughing through the waves.
Drake was fearful to alarm her too soon, and he
resolved to wait until nightfall. He lowered his
sails, filled some empty wine skins with water, and
trailed them over the side of his vessel in order to
slacken its speed. Then, as soon as the light had
faded from sea and sky, he set sail again and raced up
to the galleon. One shot from his guns terrified
the Spanish sailors into submission. As soon as they
heard the name of Drake they offered no resistance,

and Drake found himself in possession of a veritable floating treasure-house. A mass of gold and silver and a great store of emeralds, pearls, diamonds, and other precious stones were transferred to the hold of the *Golden Hind*. So much wealth had never sailed in an English ship before, and there is no wonder that by this time Drake pronounced himself to be "greatly satisfied."

He now decided to return home, but not by the way he had come. At that time men thought that there was a north-west passage round North America into the Atlantic Ocean. It was by this passage that Drake proposed to make his way back to England. He proceeded north as far as Vancouver, but the weather was too terrible to allow him to go farther. The vessel was ice-bound, the rigging was frozen, and Drake and his crew were half dead with cold. At last Drake gave up the struggle and turned his vessel southwards. Then he made the daring resolve to return home by China and the Cape of Good Hope. It was no light resolve. Twenty thousand miles lay between the *Golden Hind* and the "white walls" of England. Never before had the keel of an English ship traversed the waters lying before them, and they had no charts for their guidance. But Drake trusted to Providence, to his own genius, and to the bravery of his crew.

The story of this homeward journey is too long to tell fully in these pages. After many strange adventures, and with an occasional fight with a Spanish merchant-ship on the coast of California, they sailed straight across the Pacific to the Molucca Islands. Here they tarried for a while to repair their ship, and then on again they went along the coast of Java and into the Indian Ocean. They encountered terrible storms, and once they were cast upon a coral reef. This last adventure nearly caused their destruction, but fortunately for Francis Drake the wind changed and lifted his vessel off the rocks, so that he was able to continue his course.

At last the Cape of Good Hope was reached, and then all was easy sailing. In the autumn of 1580 the *Golden Hind*, clogged with seaweed and battered by wind and waves, sailed slowly into Plymouth Sound. Francis Drake was home again, and he brought with him not only a vast store of treasure, but the honour of being the first Englishman to sail round the world.

When the news became known in England that Francis Drake was home again, the whole country was filled with rejoicing. For more than a year no news had been heard of him, and he had long ago been given up for dead, or in the hands of the Spaniards. When the story of his marvellous adventures became known, there was hardly a man in England who did not regard him as the greatest hero of his time. Queen Elizabeth hesitated at first how to receive this man who had given such heavy blows to the honour of Spain. King Philip of Spain demanded that Drake should be punished, and that the treasure of the *Golden Hind* should be restored to Spain. But although Queen Elizabeth wished to avoid open war with Spain, she could not conceal her admiration for the daring and courage of Francis Drake. On the 4th March

1581, the Queen went down to Deptford, where the *Golden Hind* had been hauled ashore. Here she partook of a banquet on board that weather-beaten vessel, and to show her admiration for the man who had sailed round the world she gave him the honour of knighthood.

SINGEING THE KING OF SPAIN'S BEARD.

Shortly after Drake's return home, the outward peace between England and Spain threatened to break down at any moment. It was now well known by Queen Elizabeth and her statesmen that the King of Spain was getting together a great fleet in order to invade England as soon as he was ready to declare war. In 1585 he encouraged a number of English vessels to carry corn to his provinces which were stricken with famine, but no sooner did they enter his ports than he seized every one of them. When the news of this treachery reached England, the whole country clamoured for revenge against the Spaniards. Queen Elizabeth, however, did not think that England was yet prepared to declare war against such a powerful enemy as Spain. Nevertheless she was burning to be revenged, and she turned to Drake and his fellow seamen who she knew would satisfy her desire if she gave them leave.

Drake was always ready to come to blows with the Spaniards, and he was rejoiced when the queen gave him secret orders to lead another expedition to the West Indies. He was soon hard at work in Plymouth dockyard, fitting out vessels and collecting men. There was no lack of volunteers. From all parts of the country came gentlemen of England ready to sail to any quarter of the globe with such a hero as Francis Drake. Steadily and quietly the preparations went on, until at last, one fine morning in September, 1585, Drake hoisted a signal flag to the top of his mainmast. Then followed the hauling up of the sails and the weighing of anchors, and a splendid fleet sailed slowly out of Plymouth Sound, followed by the cheers of a crowd of worthy citizens.

The Spaniards soon heard that *El Draque*— the dragon—was once more unchained, and they trembled for their lives and property. It was not long before they had reason for their fear. One morning the inhabitants of the port of Vigo, on the coast of Spain, descried a fleet of strange vessels approaching the harbour. The Spanish governor, greatly astonished, sent out a boat to enquire who they were and what they wanted. Shortly afterwards the boat returned with the news that it was *El Draque* himself, who demanded the release of some English merchants who had been wrongly imprisoned. At the name of Drake, the Spanish governor instantly ordered the release of the prisoners, and when *El Draque* landed on some islands near the mouth of the harbour, the governor sent him cartloads of fruit and wine in order to keep on friendly terms with him. The following day Drake brought the whole fleet right into the harbour, and moored it close to the town. The Spanish citizens were terrified, but Drake had only come for water and fresh provisions. When he had obtained these, he sailed out of Vigo harbour to the Canaries, where he hoped to catch the Spanish gold-fleet on their way from the Cape de Verde Islands. Meanwhile tidings of Drake's appearance at Vigo had reached the ears of the King of Spain and his Council of State. They could hardly believe the news. Never before had such an insult been offered to the kingdom. That an English "pirate," as they called him, should dare to sail into one of Spain's own harbours was almost incredible.

But still more incredible things were to follow. Drake narrowly missed capturing the Spanish fleet, but he consoled himself for his misfortune by attacking the town of St. Iago. The governor and most of the people fled, and the English seamen took possession of the castle and town. There, on the 17th of November, they celebrated the birthday of Queen Elizabeth by decorating their ships in the Spanish harbour. A large quantity of rich merchandise fell into their hands, but all the gold and silver had been carried away by the inhabitants. For a fortnight they stayed in the town. It was a beautifully built city with splendid churches and public buildings, which must have filled Drake with admiration. One day, however, one of the ship boys who had strayed away was found murdered and terribly mutilated, and Drake was so enraged that he commanded his men to set the town on fire. His orders were carried out, and when the English fleet sailed away, they left behind them only smouldering ruins and ashes.

In recording this and similar actions we must not be understood as approving them. It was a cruel age, fruitful of barbarous deeds, and Drake was a

H

rough seaman who thought but little of gentleness and mercy.

Stronger and better built even than the town of St. Iago were St. Domingo and Carthagena. They were well fortified with batteries, and defended by strong forces of Spanish soldiers. It seemed impossible that a few English vessels should dare to attack such strongholds. Yet there seemed nothing which Drake feared to attempt, and wherever he went or whatever he undertook his men were ready to follow. St. Domingo and Carthagena, the strongest towns in the West Indies, fell before the invincible courage of this little band of English seamen, and the proud Spaniards had to ransom their lives and liberty by the payment of enormous sums of money.

After countless exciting adventures by land and sea, in which, as he said, he "singed the King of Spain's beard," Drake brought his fleet back to England. Here they found the whole country in a fever of excitement. The King of Spain was ready for war at last, and his great fleet, or "Invincible Armada," as he called it, lay in Cadiz harbour waiting for a favourable wind to bear it across the English Channel with thousands of Spanish soldiers.

Sir Francis Drake was allowed to take no rest. He was too great a hero to remain idle while there was work or fighting to be done. The work to be done in this case was to destroy the Armada lying in Cadiz harbour, and Queen Elizabeth and her people knew of no man more capable of carrying out such a task than Francis Drake.

IN CADIZ HARBOUR.

No longer was Drake looked upon as a privateer, a man fighting for his own private advantage. He was given the title of Her Majesty's Admiral-at-the-Seas, and a splendid fleet was placed under his command. Five large battle-ships, nine cruisers, and nine gun-boats sailed with him from Plymouth. It was the largest force that Drake had ever commanded, but even so, it was ridiculously small for the work which he was about to undertake. This was nothing less than to prevent the various divisions of Spain's great Armada from joining together, and, if possible, to burn them as they lay in their ports. If the Spanish vessels sailed for England he was to prevent them from landing.

It was a gigantic task even for a man of Drake's courage and determination, but Drake faced it like a hero. Not many days after the English warships had set sail from Plymouth they entered the bay of Cadiz. In the harbour before them lay a forest of masts. It was the great Spanish Armada which was being fitted out for the invasion of England. Drake summoned a council of war, but it was merely to tell them that he intended to attack at once. The harbour of Cadiz was exceedingly difficult to enter, on account of the rocks which encumbered its mouth. It was defended by batteries, and the Spanish war-galleys guarded the entrance. To some of the English officers it seemed sheer madness to attack such a place, but Drake had made up his mind, and most of his officers and men had perfect faith in him.

The signal was given, and the English fleet sailed straight into Cadiz harbour. A scene of wild confusion followed. Many of the Spanish ships cut their cables and tried to escape into the open sea. A number of war-galleys endeavoured to defend the entrance to the harbour, but they could only fire straight ahead, and Drake's vessels passed across them and poured upon them broadside after broadside. The English gunners had an unfailing aim. Every shot shattered some mast or spar, riddled the hulks of the galleys, or mowed down the Spanish sailors. In a short time the galleys retreated under the guns of the town batteries. Two had to be hauled ashore to prevent their sinking, and the others were strewn with the dead and dying. The troops and inhabitants of Cadiz were seized with panic and fled, leaving Drake to wreak his will upon the unprotected vessels in the harbour. Drake had no mercy. The vessels which had been intended for the invasion of England were given over to the flames, and their provisions of wine, oil, biscuits, and dried fruit were transferred to the English ships. At length Spanish troops began to pour into Cadiz to defend the city, and other Spanish galleys approached the harbour. Time after time the galleys attacked Drake, but on each occasion he beat them back, and when at last he sailed out of Cadiz harbour he left only the shattered and smouldering remnants of the Spanish fleet.

THE INVINCIBLE ARMADA.

The King of Spain had suffered a heavy loss when Drake had burned his best ships in the

THE ARMADA COMING UP THE CHANNEL. (*From an old Print.*)

harbour of Cadiz, but all the wealth of the West Indies was flowing into Philip's treasure-houses, so that he had plenty of money wherewith to build other vessels. He was eager to declare war against England, and once more he gave orders for a mighty fleet to be prepared to invade our country. He collected soldiers and sailors from all parts of Europe, and his best and bravest officers were placed in command. The preparation took many months, and even at the last, when everything was ready and the great fleet put out to sea, it was driven back again by stormy weather. At last, however, on July 19th, 1588, the fleet started once more for the coast of England.

Even the bravest Englishman might have trembled a moment for the safety of his country when he looked upon that crowd of mighty vessels which the Spaniards had named, in their pride, the "Invincible Armada," or the Unconquerable Fleet. One hundred and thirty-one vessels sailed together. They carried on board 8,000 sailors and 17,000 soldiers, with 85 surgeons and doctors and 180 priests. The Duke of Medina Sidonia was in command of the whole fleet, and his orders were to sail up the English Channel as far as Dunkirk. Here he was to take on board a great army which was awaiting his arrival. Then he was to sail into the mouth of the Thames, land his soldiers, and there remain until they had conquered England and made it one of the provinces of Spain.

In the meanwhile the people of England were watching anxiously for the arrival of the Spanish fleet, and making every preparation to resist the invasion. But the hopes of the whole nation were fastened on one man. That man was Francis Drake, who had first shown to the world that Spain, mighty as she was, could yet be made to tremble at the courage and daring of English sailors. Francis Drake himself, and indeed most Englishmen, saw that there was only one way by which England could resist the power of Spain. That way was to prevent the Spanish fleet from touching the coast of England. If once the " Invincible Armada " could land its thousands of the best and bravest soldiers in the world on English soil, the country would be in terrible danger. But England had faith in Francis Drake. Mighty as the Spanish Armada was, Englishmen were confident that the man who had burned that other Armada in Cadiz harbour could defend the white walls of England from the Spanish host and scatter their fleet to the four winds.

So Francis Drake put out to sea with a small fleet of sturdy men-of-war, and sailed up and down the English Channel, watching for the first glimpse of the Spanish sails. Day after day he paced the deck of the *Revenge* and gazed impatiently over the sea for a sight of the " Invincible Armada,' but every day his eyes met nothing but the rolling waves and the blue sky above them. Provisions began to fall short and the hungry men fell sick, but still the Armada did not come. It was waiting for a stiff south-west breeze which would bear it briskly across the Channel: but for many days there was a great calm, and hardly a breath of wind stirred the surface of the water. Drake himself thought that the Armada must have started, and he longed for a north-west breeze, so that he could meet his enemies before they had lost sight of the Spanish coast. Still the wind did not rise, and Drake and his men were half starving, for their provisions were nearly exhausted. At last, on the 19th of July, 1588, a good south-west breeze arose, and Drake's hopes were dashed to the ground. He could not advance in the teeth of the wind, and he could not remain stationary as his victuals were nearly spent, so that nothing remained but to retreat to the English port. Disappointed and angry, Drake once more appeared in the port of Plymouth, and on that same day the south-west breeze which had driven the English fleet homewards carried the "Invincible Armada" triumphantly out of the Spanish ports.

It was the captain of a small Scottish vessel who brought the news to Plymouth that the "Invincible Armada" was approaching. He had caught sight of the Spanish vessels off the Lizard, and they were sailing up the English Channel with the south-wester filling their sails.

When the Scottish captain brought his startling news, Francis Drake and the other captains of the English fleet were playing a game of bowls on Plymouth Hoe, which is a smooth green looking across the waters of Plymouth Sound. The noblest and bravest men in England surrounded Drake as he rolled the wooden balls across the green. By his side stood Walter Raleigh, Queen Elizabeth's handsome favourite. Sir Richard Grenville, a splendid old sea-hero, stood watching the game, and Lord Howard of Effingham, the Lord High Admiral of England, talked familiarly with other brave old heroes such as John Hawkins, Martin Frobisher, and John Davies.

These were the men who heard the hasty words of Captain Fleming as he told of the approach of the enemy. The Lord High Admiral wanted to start off at once, but Drake, with his usual cool courage, said, "There is time to finish the game first and beat the Spaniards afterwards." The other captains agreed with hearty laughter, and while the Spanish ships drew near, these English captains finished their game of bowls.

Then they went calmly to their ships, and with every man at his post and every heart ready to fight till death for the safety and honour of England, the English fleet sailed out of Plymouth Sound towards the Spanish fleet. The "Invincible Armada" was sweeping up the Channel in the form of a crescent, the horns of which were seven miles apart.

The English vessels lost no time in getting to close quarters with the enemy, and first and foremost was Francis Drake. The Spanish vessels were huge and unwieldy, while the English ships were light, and could tack and turn so readily that they could pour broadsides of shot into the enemy's hulks before the Spanish galleys could close with them and return their fire.

Francis Drake filled the Spanish fleet with terror. His sturdy vessel dashed across the waves towards the mightiest Spanish war-vessels, and after pouring forth a storm of shot, he would suddenly tack and speed away to deal destruction to another foe.

The Duke of Medina Sidonia, who commanded

the Spanish Armada, obeyed the king's orders and avoided a general battle in order to reach Dunkirk, where a large Spanish army was waiting to reinforce him. The English fleet followed him closely, and they were joined by another fleet under Lord Seymour. When, however, the Spaniards reached Dunkirk, they would not venture out to sea again. Drake and his fellow captains were anxious to get them out at any cost, and they at last hit upon a plan to do so. That plan was to send fire ships into the midst of the Spanish fleet. Drake offered one of his own ships, and seven more were chosen for the sacrifice. They were filled with tar, powder, and oil, so that they would burn fiercely, and two brave captains, Young and Prowse, volunteered to lead them close to the Spanish vessels and to set them on fire.

Shortly after midnight, in the absolute darkness of sea and sky, the eight vessels floated towards the Spanish galleons, as they lay tossing at anchor. Suddenly a great blaze of light started out of the darkness, and it was followed by another and another until eight piles of flame moved across the waves towards the Spanish ships. They knew that *El Draque* had been at work. A great panic took possession of them. With shouts of horror and dismay they cut their cables, and ship after ship was borne by the wind out to sea, crashing against one another like a herd of frightened cattle. The fire-ships had missed their aim, and not a single Spanish vessel had been set alight. Nevertheless the desired effect was achieved, for the "Invincible Armada" was flying out to sea in wild confusion.

Now Drake took the lead, and dashed after the

Spaniards. The *Revenge* bore down silently upon the *San Martin*, the flag-ship of the Duke of Medina Sidonia. Not until they were within pistol shot did Drake allow his men to fire. Then a terrible broadside was hurled into the Spanish ship. As it staggered from the blow, and a cloud of smoke enveloped the *Revenge*, Drake passed on to another group of Spanish galleons and dealt with them in the same way. Behind him followed Frobisher in the *Triumph* and Hawkins in the *Victory*, and with these old Devonshire comrades Drake shattered the mightiest of the enemy's warships. The Spaniards did not lack for courage. They fought as bravely as Francis Drake himself. Although the English ships tacked round about them with marvellous celerity, and the English gunners cannonaded their vessels with deadly effect, the Spaniards would not think of surrender. But, at last, when their ammunition was exhausted, when many of their vessels had sunk and their decks were strewn with dead and dying, they saw that all hope was lost, and the admiral gave the signal for retreat.

The English captains had also run out of powder and shot, so that they did not follow the Spaniards in their flight. But the winds and the waves now fought against the power of Spain. A fearful storm broke over the English Channel and the North Sea. The Spanish Armada could not return south to Spain, but was driven northward by the gale. The huge and unwieldy galleons, the remnants of that Armada which the Spaniards had so vainly called "Invincible," were dashed on the rocky coasts of Donegal, Sligo, Galway, and Kerry. Most of the vessels were shattered to pieces, and hundreds of Spanish soldiers were drowned or slaughtered by the wild Irish tribes into whose hands they fell. Less than 10,000 men returned to the country from

A REMNANT OF THE "INVINCIBLE ARMADA."

which they had set out in all the pride and magnificence of the Spanish Armada. Thanks to Francis Drake and his brave comrades, and thanks to the fury of wind and waves, England was once more in peace and safety.

THE LAST DAYS OF DRAKE.

The defeat of the Armada was the crowning incident in the life of Drake. He had now reached his highest fame and glory. His life's work was accomplished, and the events which came after are insignificant in comparison.

Other expeditions he led against the Spanish possessions in the West Indies, and he taught English ships to be familiar with those Western seas which he had been the first Englishman to explore. To the end of his days he was busy fighting against his old enemies the Spaniards, and many a Spanish galleon laden with stores of rich treasure was forced to yield to the strong hand of Francis Drake. It was in one of these expeditions that he met his death. After many wild adventures, his usual good fortune seemed to leave him. His men were beaten back by the Spaniards, many of them were stricken down by the deadly climate of the South American coast, and, to add to his danger, foul weather arose and drove his ships into the Mosquito Gulf, where he had to take shelter behind a little island. No spot in the West Indies is more lovely than the neighbourhood of the Mosquito Gulf. The foliage is rich and luxuriant, and the most gorgeous flowers seem to make the place an earthly paradise.

But this outward loveliness hides the deadly poison which rises into the atmosphere from the soil beneath. As Drake's boats sailed into the beautiful creeks in search of fresh fruit, horrible reptiles crept out of a slime, reeking with poisonous vapour. Drake's men dropped one by one, and at last Drake himself was attacked with dysentery. The wind remained contrary, and kept them close to the deadly shore. When at last it changed, and bore them out into the open sea, it came too late. The brave seaman who had never been daunted by

mortal foe was at last conquered, and he lay weak
and helpless on his death-bed. On the 28th of
January, when his vessel was anchored off Porto
Bello, he was seized with a delirium. He arose
from his bed and clothed himself, and called for
his arms with wild words, which made his comrades
shudder. Then his fury passed from him, and he
was led back to bed, and, at length, peacefully and
quietly, the hero of a hundred fights gave out his
last breath.

His body was placed in a leaden coffin and
carried a league out to sea. Then, amid trumpet
blasts and the roar of cannon, the comrades who
loved him as a hero, cast his body to the deep.
Two ships for which there was no further need
were sunk on each side of him, and then the fleet
went its way sadly, leaving their great captain
alone in his ocean grave.

V.
JOHN HAMPDEN
AND
THE DEFENCE OF ENGLISH LIBERTY.

ONE of the most important laws laid down in Magna Charta was that the king must not obtain money by tax-ing the people without the con-sent of Parlia-ment. As Simon de Montfort had wisely said, those who pay the money have a right to say how much they shall pay, and how the money shall be spent. But al-though this good law was well known to every English king, some of them disobeyed it when it suited them to do so. The Parliament was not always strong enough to defend its rights against powerful kings, and the English

JOHN HAMPDEN.

people could not always find a leader brave enough to champion their cause.

At last, in the reign of Charles I., a country gentleman, with no power in the land except that of a good name and fame, stood out from amongst his countrymen to brave the wrath of an offended king. He asserted that the English people could not lawfully be taxed without the consent of Parliament, and that no English king had a right to disobey the laws written down in Magna Charta, or in the other great charters and statutes of England. This brave gentleman and good citizen was John Hampden.

Charles I. was by no means the worst of English kings. Indeed, he possessed many good qualities which fitted him to wear the English crown with dignity. Unfortunately his conduct in the public affairs of his kingdom was not at all in keeping with the virtue of his private life. He was untruthful, obstinate and narrow-minded; he made promises which he broke as soon as made, and, above all, he had no respect for the old laws and liberties of the English people, which he had promised to preserve. He soon aroused the displeasure of his people by taxing them without the consent of Parliament. The Parliament issued a protest, but the king ignored it and committed some of the members to prison. In this way he was twice guilty of breaking the laws of the country, for in Magna Charta it is laid down that "no Freeman shall be taken or imprisoned unless by the lawful judgment of his peers or by the law of the land," and, again, that "no scutage or aid shall be imposed in our kingdom except by the Common Council of the Realm."

When Charles sent out his sheriffs and officers to collect the illegal tax called tunnage and poundage, most of the people paid the money because they

CHARLES I.
(From the Mezzotint of J. Smith, after Van Dyck.)

did not dare offend the king. One man, however there was who was bold enough to stand up for his country's rights. When John Hampden, a Buckinghamshire squire, was summoned to pay his share of the money demanded by the king, he refused to give a farthing. When he was asked the reason of his refusal he answered calmly and fearlessly that he was afraid to bring down a curse upon himself by disobeying Magna Charta. For this brave answer he was immediately arrested, and closely imprisoned.

The man who thus took upon himself to challenge the tyranny of the king was previously without fame. His personal friends knew him as a country gentleman who led a quiet and peaceful life upon his large estates in Buckinghamshire, and as a hard-working Member of Parliament who had never attracted any great public attention.

John Hampden was born in 1594, in the reign of James I. He was descended from a good old Buckinghamshire family, and inherited his father's estates at an early age. He was educated at the grammar school of Thame, and afterwards, when he was fifteen years of age, he went to Magdalen College in the University of Oxford, where he gained some distinction. When he was nineteen years old he became a student of law at the Inner Temple, London, and he studied with so much diligence that he became thoroughly acquainted with all the principles of English law.

At this time of his life, when he was in the first glow and buoyancy of young manhood, he entered a good deal into the pleasures of life, but as he became older and more thoughtful a change took place in his character. "On a sudden," says the historian Clarendon, "from a life of great pleasure and licence, he retired to extraordinary sobriety and strictness, to a more reserved and melancholy society." At this time he married

Elizabeth Symeon, a lady of great virtue, to whom he was passionately attached. There is no doubt that in the peaceful pleasures of home-life he learnt to despise the folly and viciousness of King James's Court. He retired to his estates in Buckinghamshire and spent his days in domestic peace, cultivating the land, and adding to his stock of learning by reading the great masters of literature.

Yet, in spite of the change in his character, "he preserved," says Clarendon, "his own natural cheerfulness and vivacity, and, above all, a flowing courtesy to all men."

After a while he came to see that he had a higher duty in life than the cultivation of his estates and the acquisition of learning. He felt that he ought to take a share in the public work of the country, and for this purpose he entered Parliament. He took his seat in the House of Commons in January, 1621, as member for Wendover. From that time forward he devoted himself to the interests of his country. He did not endeavour to attract public notice by great speeches, but he was always to be found in his place, ready to vote in a good cause, and working quietly and industriously. At last, as we have seen, he was bold enough to incur the king's wrath by refusing to pay the money which was illegally demanded without the consent of Parliament.

He was kept a prisoner for some time at a place in Hampshire, until the king, wishing to win back the favour of the people, ordered his release. In the meanwhile, however, King Charles was still further enraging the English people by his unlawful and tyrannical actions. At last he could not obtain sufficient money by illegal means, and he was obliged to summon another Parliament to grant him a fresh supply. In 1628 the Parliament assembled once more, and John Hampden was again a member for the borough of Wendover.

No sooner had the Parliament met than they immediately called upon the king to redress the grievances which afflicted the nation. They drew up a famous document, called the Petition of Right, which required the king to raise no taxes without the consent of Parliament, to imprison no man for refusing to pay unjust taxes, or without a trial, and to put a stop to the many illegal practices which he had permitted.

After much delay and great objection on the part of the king, he was obliged to give his assent to that famous Petition of Right. But now the Parliament and English people began to learn the value of the king's word. No sooner had he given his most sacred and solemn promise to obey the articles of the Petition than he ignored almost all of them.

When Parliament next met they were in no good humour with the king. They made an enquiry into the matter of tunnage and poundage, and summoned the officers of the Custom House to the bar of the House of Commons to be examined. One of the members, Sir John Eliot, an intimate friend of Hampden, denounced the tax as being contrary to the English law, and requested the House of Commons to pass a resolution to that effect. The Speaker, however, disgracing himself by forgetting the privileges of Parliament, said that the king had commanded him to put no such question to the vote.

At these words a violent and extraordinary scene took place. The door of the House of Commons was

THE SPEAKER HELD DOWN IN HIS CHAIR.

locked, members denounced the disgraceful words which had been uttered by the Speaker, and two of them, named Valentine and Hollis, held the Speaker down in his chair by main force while Sir John Eliot's resolution was read, amidst loud shouts and a great tumult.

Shortly after this scene King Charles dissolved

Parliament, and he once more broke the assent which he had given to the Petition of Right, by throwing Sir John Eliot and several other members of Parliament into prison.

John Hampden again retired into the country, and for eleven years, during which the kingdom remained without a Parliament, he spent his days in study and rural duties on his Buckinghamshire estate. From this peaceful retreat he wrote many letters of consolation and advice to his unfortunate and noble friend Sir John Eliot. These letters are still preserved, and are beautiful examples of the piety, wisdom, affection, and true nobility of John Hampden.

During the eleven years which followed the dissolution of Parliament, Charles I. continued his evil course. He made a favourite of Thomas Wentworth, Earl of Strafford, a man of great ability, but with a cruel, unprincipled, and hateful character. He was appointed Lord Lieutenant of Ireland, where he committed a great number of crimes and governed with abominable cruelty and injustice. He was the worst counsellor whom Charles could have chosen, and he urged the king to do without Parliament altogether, and to govern the country by means of a powerful army.

Prompted by Sir W. Noy, Attorney-General, King Charles resolved to put a new tax upon his people. This tax was called " ship-money," because it required the principal towns and counties of England to provide money for building ships of war. Never before had the inland counties of England been called upon to furnish ships. It was well known also that it was called "ship-money" for a pretext, and that the money would really find its way into the king's private treasury. But beyond this, it was utterly illegal, for it was demanded without the consent of Parliament, and was therefore a violation of the Petition of Right. At this new tyranny on the part of the king, the people of England were filled with excitement and anger, but as yet they did not dare to break out in open remonstrance.

One man, however, was bold enough to resist this fresh injustice. The champion of English liberty was again John Hampden, who refused to pay a penny of the twenty shillings which was demanded from him as his share of the "ship-money." It must be clearly understood that Hampden did not resist the tax because he did not want to part with the money. He was, indeed, a wealthy man, and twenty shillings would have made no difference to his worldly comfort. He refused to pay it because he determined to uphold the English law against a tyrant. He knew that if he refused he would be brought to trial, and he hoped that his judges would be honest enough to declare that the king had acted contrary to the law of the land.

When the English people heard that one man had been found bold enough to resist the payment of "ship-money," John Hampden became a hero in their eyes. "Till this time," says Clarendon, "he was rather of reputation in his own country than of public discourse or fame in the kingdom; but then he grew the argument of all tongues, every man inquiring who and what he was that durst, at his own charge, support the liberty and prosperity of the kingdom."

When the case came up before the Court of Exchequer, the whole nation waited anxiously for the decision of the judges. At last they gave their judgment. Five of the judges were in favour of Hampden. The remaining seven said that the king was in the right. Of course the majority decided the case, and John Hampden was ordered to pay the tax.

Like an honourable citizen, John Hampden paid the money. He had appealed to the law, but when he found that the law had declared against him, he obeyed the judgment loyally. Nevertheless he knew that the seven judges had given this decision because they were afraid of the king's anger, and he resolved to prove in spite of them that the king had no power to tax the people without the consent of Parliament.

Indeed, although the majority of judges had decided against him, he had kindled a spirit of resistance in the nation. "The judgment," says Clarendon, "proved of more advantage and credit to the gentleman condemned than to the king's service." Also, during the trial he had shown so much courage, good sense, patriotism, and modesty that, instead of being an unknown country gentleman as before, his reputation now reached a great height, and he became the most popular man in the country.

When Parliament was again summoned, John Hampden took his place as member for Buckinghamshire, and from that day until his death he devoted himself with all his heart and strength to the interests of his country.

Lord Clarendon, who favoured the cause of King

Charles, has left a remarkable testimony to the ability and noble character of his political opponent, John Hampden:—

"When the Parliament began (being returned knight of the shire for the county where he lived) the

THE ARREST OF STRAFFORD.

eyes of all men were fixed on him as their *patriæ pater*, and the pilot that must steer the vessel through the tempests and rocks which threatened it. And I am persuaded his power and interest at that time was greater to do good or hurt than any man's in the kingdom, or than any man of his rank hath had in any time; for his reputation of honesty was universal, and his affections seemed so publicly guided that no corrupt or private ends could bias them."

No sooner had the Parliament met than it immediately endeavoured to redress some of those grievances under which the country was groaning. The first action of the members was to impeach Thomas Wentworth, Earl of Strafford, on a charge of high treason. He was brought up to the bar of the House of Commons, and charged with the many acts of tyranny and wrongdoing which he had committed in Ireland and elsewhere. The earl pleaded that he had acted with the consent and encouragement of King Charles. There was, indeed, some truth in this, but it did not save the king's minister from meeting the punishment which the Parliament considered due to his crimes. King Charles disgraced himself for ever by deserting his favourite in the hour of his need, and he signed the death-warrant of the man who had served him only too faithfully.

This Parliament, which was called the "Long Parliament," because it remained in power for nineteen years, continued the work of redressing the nation's grievances. Gradually, however, many of the members relented towards King Charles. They thought they had been too severe with him, and that, as he was king, he had a right to behave in what manner it pleased him. By degrees the House of Commons was divided into two parties—those who thought the king ought to have more liberty of action, and those who could no longer trust the king when they remembered how often he had broken his most solemn promises. The leader of the latter party was John Hampden. He and his comrades saw that the king was still continuing in his evil ways, and that he was determined not to respect the advice of his Parliament or the law of the land. They drew up an address which has become famous under the name of the Grand Remonstrance. In this remonstrance they set forth all the unjust and illegal actions which had been committed during the preceding fifteen years, and in conclusion they entreated the king to employ ministers in whom the Parliament could confide.

A stormy debate took place in Parliament when John Hampden and his friends presented the Grand Remonstrance to be sanctioned by the House of Commons. So great was the excitement and so divided the opinions of the members that many of them were on the point of assaulting each other. An eye-witness of this violent scene relates that "We had sheathed our swords in each other's bowels had not the sagacity and great calmness of Mr. Hampden prevented it."

The debate lasted from nine in the morning of the 21st of November, 1640, until two o'clock on the following morning. In conclusion, the Grand Remonstrance was passed by a majority of only nine.

Shortly after the passing of this address, the king added one more crime and folly to the long list which had already gained him the hatred of half the nation

On January 3rd, 1642, without a word of warning, he sent down the Attorney-General to the House of Commons to arrest John Hampden and five other gentlemen of the Commons on a charge of high treason. The king had no power by law to order this arrest, because the only way in which the members of the House of Commons could be charged with high treason was by a Bill issued by a grand jury.

The Commons rightly refused to give up any of the members. This refusal was followed by another criminal act on the part of the king, which not only aroused the fury of the people to an ungovernable pitch, but filled the king's own friends with sorrow and indignation.

The king resolved to go to Parliament with an armed force, and to seize John Hampden and his comrades, even at the cost of their blood, on the very floor of that House which guarded the liberties and laws of the English nation. It was one of the worst crimes a king could commit, and the last action which a nation could patiently endure.

On the day appointed for this infamous deed, the king left his palace of Whitehall, attended by a body of two hundred pikemen and a large number of courtiers armed with swords and pistols. In this manner he proceeded to Westminster Hall, where the Parliament was sitting. At the southern entrance his guard divided, and formed into two lines on either side of the hall. The king walked between them, and knocked at the door of the House of Commons. Then he entered and walked up to the Speaker's chair. As he did so the members rose to their feet and uncovered their heads, gazing at the king in absolute silence, with looks of profound sorrow at his insult to them and the disgrace he was bringing upon his own name.

"By your leave, Mr. Speaker," said the king, "I must borrow your chair for a while."

Speaker Lenthall fell upon his knee while the

king took his seat in the chair. Charles glanced hastily round the House at the places where Hampden and his comrades usually sat. But they were not there. They had received an early notice of the king's intention, and had withdrawn from the House. The king questioned the Speaker as to their absence, but Speaker Lenthall replied that he had "neither eyes to see nor tongue to speak, but according to the direction of the gentlemen of the Commons."

"Well," said the king, "since I do see the birds are flown, I do expect, as soon as they return, you do send them to me."

Thereupon he left the chair, and darting angry glances upon the silent assembly, he retired from the House while some of the bolder members called out "Privilege! privilege!" meaning thereby that the king had insulted the rights and privileges of the Commons.

The news of this outrage spread like wildfire through the city of London, and thence over the whole country, rousing the people to a great excitement and anger.

That night the citizens of London were in arms. On the following day the shops were shut, crowds of armed citizens paraded the streets, and surrounded the king's coach with threatening shouts and insults.

In a few days the House of Commons showed their contempt for the king's action by summoning John Hampden and his comrades to attend their places in Parliament, and to resume their duties.

With great rejoicing and enthusiasm on the part

of the citizens of London, the five members were
conducted back to Parliament.   King Charles did
not remain in London to witness the triumph of
the people.   On the preceding day, accompanied
by a few attendants, he fled secretly from the palace
and Whitehall, which he was only to see again

WESTMINSTER HALL IN THE TIME OF CHARLES I.

when he should step from one of its windows on
to a scaffold prepared for his execution.

The Parliament was now in no mood to listen
to his haughty words or false promises.   They
demanded that he should give them the right to
appoint the officers for the militia, so that the
military power of the kingdom should be in their
hands.   The king refused.   The Commons thereupon ignored his refusal, and appointed the officers.

Things had now come to such a pass that unless one side gave way the question would have to be decided at the cost of bloodshed. Neither party would yield, and both prepared to fight. At last, on the 23rd of April, 1642, Sir John Hotham, in command at Hull, refused to give up the arms and powder magazine to the king, and closed the gates of the town against the king's forces. This was the first act of war, and it was followed by that terrible Great Rebellion, when Englishmen fought against Englishmen and brother against brother, until the country was bathed in blood.

On one side was the king and his "Cavaliers," and on the other the Parliament and the people. The Cavaliers were composed of the noblemen and gentry of England, who fought for what they believed to be the truth, and for what they believed to be honour. They forgot, or did not realise, the crimes of Charles I., and they looked upon him with loyal-hearted devotion, as the noble king of a rebellious nation, as their lord and master, for whom they were bound if necessary to sacrifice their property and their lives. On the other side were the Parliament and the citizens, who could not forget the falsehood, the tyranny, the disgraceful conduct of Charles, and who were resolved themselves to die rather than let the liberties of the nation be trampled under foot by a tyrant.

Needless to say, John Hampden, who had already been the champion of English liberty, was one of the leaders of the popular cause.

He gave two thousand pounds towards the public service, and took a colonel's commission in the army. He went into his native county of Buckingham to raise a regiment for the Parliament, and his neighbours flocked to his standard.

Hampden himself gained the admiration of his comrades, and even of his enemies, by his energy, his great military skill, and his heroic courage. In every fight he was always to be found at the post of danger; in every council of war he was the wisest counsellor.

His party did not long enjoy the benefit of his knowledge and courage. He was struck down in one of the early fights. It was at Chalgrove Field. Prince Rupert, the nephew of King Charles, had made a dash out of Oxford with a regiment of cavalry, and was burning the villages in the hands of the Parliamentarians, and killing the troops quartered in them. Hampden sent an urgent message to the Earl of Essex, in command of the Parliamentary forces, to attack Prince Rupert's cavalry and prevent them returning to Oxford. In the meanwhile he himself set out, with all the cavalry he could gather together, to check Prince Rupert until the Earl of Essex had time to approach. He came up with the Royalist forces on the field of Chalgrove.

Hampden led the attack. A fierce struggle took place, but in the first charge Hampden was mortally wounded. His arms dropped powerless by his side, and his head fell forward over his horse's neck. Shortly afterwards he was seen riding off the field while the fight was still in progress. He rode towards his father-in-law's house, which stood close by. From this house he had carried away his bride

HAMPDEN MORTALLY WOUNDED AT CHALGROVE FIELD.

on his marriage day, many years before. The remembrance of that happy day must have passed across his mind as he looked upon the house with dying eyes. He tried to reach it, but a body of Prince Rupert's horse lay between him and the house, so that he had to turn aside. He reached a brook which divided him from the village of Thame. For a while he paused, half fainting with the agony of his wound. Then, with a sudden effort, he clapped spurs to his horse and leaped the brook. At last, clinging feebly to his horse, he reached a friend's house.

He knew that his life was fast ebbing away, but with heroic courage and patriotism he dictated letters from his deathbed to the Parliamentary leaders, giving them good counsel for the conduct of the war. For six days he lingered in cruel agony, and then, on the 24th of June, 1643, his brave spirit passed away.

His last words were a prayer for the welfare of the country he had served so faithfully.

"O Lord," he murmured, "save my bleeding country. Have these realms in Thy special keeping. . . Let the king see his error, and turn the hearts of his wicked counsellors from the malice and wickedness of their designs."

Such was the life of John Hampden, one of the bravest and best of English gentlemen.

He died too soon for his country's welfare, for those who carried on his work were led astray by passion and self-interest. But he lived long enough to proclaim the liberty of Englishmen, and to gain an imperishable fame.

J

VI.

ADMIRAL BLAKE

AND

THE SUPREMACY AT SEA.

THE great Lord Clarendon, who has given us the most vivid word-portraits of the principal characters of the time of Charles I., the Commonwealth and the Restoration, has summed up the greatness of Admiral Blake in the following words:—

"He was the first that infused that proportion of courage into the seamen by making them see by experience what mighty things they could do if they were resolved, and taught them to fight *in fire* as well as upon water."

When we have read the life of Francis Drake we cannot agree with Lord Clarendon that Admiral Blake was the *first* man to teach English seamen "what mighty things they could do if they were resolved." There is no doubt, however, that Blake was one of the greatest admirals who has ever defeated England's enemies at sea, and some of his exploits are as worthy of the admiration of Englishmen as any that have made famous the names of Drake or Nelson.

Strange to say, this great man who defeated the boldest and most experienced admirals of Spain and Holland, did not set foot on board ship until he was forty-nine years of age. His early manhood was spent, like that of John Hampden, in the

peaceful cultivation of his family estates. Like
Hampden, too, he left these rural duties to take
up arms against those whom he believed to be the
enemies of his country's liberty — against King
Charles and his Cavaliers. In the lamentable Civil

ADMIRAL BLAKE.

(From the Painting in Greenwich Hospital.)

War which cost Charles his head, Blake proved
himself to be a brave and skilful fighter on land
before he was called upon to do battle at sea.

Robert Blake was born in the year 1599. He
belonged to a well-to-do Somersetshire family, and
when his father died in 1625 he inherited the family
estate of Knoll Hill, Bridgwater, and with it the
duty of providing for his numerous brothers and

sisters. In 1640 he was elected member of Parliament for Bridgwater, and, like John Hampden, to whom we have already compared him, he gained a reputation more by his industry and quiet, plodding work than by brilliant rhetoric or daring actions. When the Civil War broke out Blake took the side of the Parliament, and from that time until his death he never swerved in his fidelity to that cause, and to the Protector, Oliver Cromwell. He was chiefly responsible for the defence of the West of England against the Royalists, and his defence of Taunton, which was besieged by the king's forces for many months, was one of the most brilliant achievements during the Civil War.

Blake had won a great reputation as a skilful general, but the defence of Taunton was the last service he performed on land. On February 24th, 1648, the Parliament appointed him to be "admiral of the fleet now at sea."

Nowadays we should think it extraordinary if an officer of the army were suddenly appointed to command a ship. In Blake's time, however, this was a usual occurrence. The ships were *navigated* by men like Francis Drake or old John Hawkins, who had lived all their lives upon the sea, but they were often *commanded* by men whose only knowledge of seamanship consisted in making straight for the enemy.

Yet there is no doubt that it is a good thing for the commander of a ship to have received his education in rough winds and weather, and that he should know every rope and pulley of the vessel he commands, and every current and shallow of the sea he sails. These are the kind of men who have carried the British flag into every nook of the wide world, and who have done such mighty service in the building up of the British Empire. Yet it is all the more credit to Robert Blake that, in spite of being a country gentleman and a soldier until he was forty-nine years of age, he should have become one of the greatest of English admirals.

His first duty at sea was to shatter the naval forces of the Royalists. They were commanded by Prince Rupert, and although they were not powerful enough to restore the fallen fortunes of the king, they were a serious source of mischief to the cause of the Parliament by capturing merchant vessels in the Channel.

CHASING PRINCE RUPERT.

Blake sailed under orders to sink and burn Prince Rupert's ships, whenever and wherever he might come upon them. The prince, however, did not mean to be caught easily, and he played a game of hide and seek with the new admiral. For a time Blake kept him imprisoned in Kinsale harbour, but when bad weather obliged Blake to withdraw his ships from the coast, Rupert slipped out of the harbour with his seven vessels, and, escaping from the clutches of his enemy, sailed off for the coast of Portugal. Here he took refuge in Lisbon harbour, sheltered by the Portuguese guns, which were friendly to his cause. Blake soon followed him and blockaded the harbour. Then a series of attacks began on either side, but Blake did not venture to enter the harbour in face of the guns of Portugal, and Prince Rupert would not leave his shelter.

At last Blake informed the King of Portugal that if he did not give the guests in his harbour notice to quit, he would seize the Brazilian fleet which was on its way home to Portugal. This threat only put the king and his ministers into a

PRINCE RUPERT.
(*From the Portrait by Van Dyck.*)

great rage. They equipped some ships and asked Prince Rupert to help them to revenge themselves on Blake. Rupert was quite willing to do so, but the Portuguese sailors turned out to be cowards and would not fight.

Blake now carried his words into action.

The Brazilian fleet, suspecting no danger, sailed on its homeward journey, laden with sugar and other valuable cargo. When it was within five miles of Lisbon harbour, Blake sailed out to meet it and gave it a warm greeting. After a feeble resistance from the Portuguese merchants, one vessel was sunk and a dozen captured. King John of Portugal now saw that it was high time to get rid of the visitors who had been the cause of all this trouble. By threats or bribes he persuaded the Royalists to leave Lisbon, and one day they sneaked out of the harbour and gave Blake the slip.

Once more followed a game of hide-and-seek. At last, in November, 1650, Blake caught the Royalist fleet at Carthagena. Prince Rupert was now in a desperate plight. His ships were manned to a large extent by men whom he had captured from English merchant ships. Naturally they did not make much of a resistance against their own friends, although the Royalists threatened to shoot them if they did not fight. Blake attacked them with great energy, and soon succeeded in capturing the whole fleet. He was bitterly disappointed, however, when he found that Prince Rupert was not among his prisoners. The prince had been separated from his fleet when Blake had attacked them, and once more he succeeded in escaping. Nevertheless Blake had carried out his task success-fully, for the Royalists no longer possessed a navy

THE WAR WITH HOLLAND

Up to this time, although Blake had shown him-self a capable naval commander, he had done nothing to achieve a great fame. His fights with Prince Rupert and the Portuguese were against an enemy of no great power. But now he had an opportunity of proving his skill against the greatest admirals and the best sailors of Europe. In 1652 war broke out with Holland, and Blake found himself matched against Admirals Van Tromp and De Ruyter and the Dutch fleets which had won glory in many hard-fought fights.

There were many causes which led up to the war with Holland. In the seventeenth century the Dutch had gradually taken the place which the Spaniards held the century before. Their ships sailed into every sea and traded with every port. The Dutch traders had driven the English out of the Spice Islands in the West Indies. Worse than this, Dutch fishermen sailed their fleets into English waters, guarded by armed vessels, and fished openly without paying the lawful taxes. This behaviour naturally stirred up the blood of every skipper and fisherman from Yarmouth to Land's End. Even the English Government was at last roused to take action against these grievances. Parliament passed a Navigation Act, which forbade any goods to be imported into England except on English vessels, or the vessels of the countries from which they came. This Act was likely to do a great deal of damage to Holland, as Dutch vessels possessed the greatest "carrying trade" in Europe. A fire was smouldering between the two countries, waiting only for a spark in order to burst into flames.

In May of the year 1652 an encounter took place

between Admirals Blake and Van Tromp which decided the question of war.

The Dutch admiral was cruising off the coast of Holland for the purpose of protecting the Dutch merchant vessels and keeping a watch on the movements of the English fleet. Blake was quietly biding his time with fifteen good vessels in the Dover Roads, while eight others were lying in the Downs. On May 19th Tromp moved into the English Channel, and here he fell in with a countryman of his own who brought him news of a Dutch vessel which had been fired upon by an English ship. This was quite enough for Admiral Tromp, who was burning for some pretext to practise his men's gunnery on the English fleet. Without hesitation, he crowded on sail and swept down the English Channel towards Dover.

Admiral Blake, standing on board the *James*, soon caught sight of the Dutch sails, and guessed their purpose at once. War had not yet been formally declared between England and Holland, but with every Dutch gunner and every English tar itching to get at close quarters, that little fact was quite ignored. Admiral Blake ordered the decks to be cleared for action, the guns were loosed from their cordage, and the gunners stood by their iron monsters with the burning fuses in their hands and the powder-monkeys ready at their sides. Admiral Tromp's vessel, the *Brederode*, was the first to open fire. A broadside came crashing over the water and whistled through the English rigging. Blake was not slow with his answer, and before the first boom of the Dutch cannon had died away, there was a roar **from**

the English fleet.   Now the battle began in earnest.
Blake, desperately eager to get alongside a Dutch-
man, outsailed the rest of his squadron, and his ship,
the *James*, attacked the whole of the Dutch fleet
single-handed.   Instantly he was surrounded by a

IN THE DOWNS.

crowd of enemies.   A storm of shot swept upon
the English vessel.   Her mainmast crashed overboard, her sails were torn into shreds, her hull
was scored and battered by a hailstorm of bullets.
Fifty of her men strewed the decks in dead or dying
heaps.   The master of the ship himself was killed.
In the meantime the other vessels of the English
fleet had come up and tackled the Dutchmen with

bull-dog courage. The battle raged for five hours, from four o'clock in the afternoon to nine o'clock in the evening. The English were outnumbered, and seemed likely to get the worst of the job, until relief was brought by the commander of the eight ships which had been lying at anchor in the Downs. He had heard the thunder of the guns, and set all sail to come up to the scene of action. At nine o'clock he brought his eight ships in touch with the Dutch fleet, and cut off two of their vessels. Soon afterwards Admiral Tromp ordered a retreat and, covered by the darkness of the night, sailed off to the Flemish coast. For the first time in his life he had found an equal in courage and naval skill. The honours of war remained with Admiral Blake, who could pride himself upon having beaten off the most renowned admiral in command of the most experienced fleet of Europe.

The news of this encounter set all England ablaze with a desire for war, and accordingly it was formally declared against Holland.

Blake found plenty of work to do in the Channel, where he had been ordered to give a "friendly" reception to the Dutch merchant vessels who were coming home from all parts of the globe. They were blissfully ignorant as yet that war had broken out with England, and sailed peacefully down the Channel on their way home. Of course, they popped right into the hands of the English fleet waiting for them in Dover Downs, and many a richly laden vessel was captured by Admiral Blake and his comrades and sent up the Thames. Blake now swept round the north coast of Scotland and captured the Dutch herring fleet. The ships of war that had guarded it were sunk or taken, the herring cargoes were tossed into the sea, and the fishing-smacks were left to find their way home again empty-handed. Van Tromp fell into disgrace for not defending this fleet, and two other admirals, De Witt and De Ruyter, were appointed to succeed him in command of the Dutch fleet.

Blake was not long in becoming acquainted with these gentlemen. In September of 1652 they took up their position close to the Goodwin Sands, in full view of the English fleet, which was lying in the Downs. Of course, this was a challenge to fight, and Blake was not the man to refuse it. But the Dutch had cleverly put themselves in an advantageous position. Their vessels were more flat-bottomed than the English, so that they could sail in shallower water. They had crept close to the Goodwin Sands, where it is extremely dangerous and difficult to navigate. The wind was blowing from the Sands, and if the English vessels sailed outside the Dutch fleet they would be at a great disadvantage. On the other hand, if they tried to get between the enemy and the Goodwins, they would be in great danger of grounding their vessels on the sand.

Admiral Blake resolved to take the latter course, and chance the danger. At four o'clock in the afternoon he sailed towards the enemy, and the whole English fleet passed between the Dutchmen and the Sands.

As they passed they opened fire, and every vessel thundered a broadside at the enemy. They did not avoid, however, the dangers of the Sands. Two of the English vessels went aground. Fortunately not much damage was done, for in a short while the wind blew them off the Sands again, and their fate served as a warning to the rest of the fleet. Admiral Blake now ordered his ships to close upon the enemy, and the battle began in earnest. Hull to hull, and yard-arm to yard-arm, each English ship grappled an enemy. The fighting was hard on both sides, but the fortune of war remained with the English. Several Dutch ships were sunk, and others were shattered and splintered so that not a mast remained standing. Once more the Dutch availed themselves of the darkness to escape from the English guns. On the following morning they were six miles away, and Admiral Blake was unable to get within firing distance before they ran under the shelter of the coast of Holland.

This defeat under the Admirals De Ruyter and De Witt made the Dutch turn again to the old hero, Van Tromp. Once again he was placed in chief command, and now a long and deadly duel took place between the Dutch admiral and the English rival of his fame. On November 29th another battle was fought within sight of the Goodwin Sands. The Dutch outnumbered the English by more than forty men-of-war, but Blake attacked them with his usual daring. The English were defeated, but it was no disgrace to have fought for five hours against such a hero as Van Tromp, when he had two vessels to one of the English.

Early in the following year, Blake heard that his old enemy, Van Tromp, was coming up the Channel in guard of a mighty squadron of merchant vessels richly laden with produce from the West Indies.

With a small fleet of about a dozen vessels, Blake
started out to give battle to this powerful enemy.
When he caught sight of them the merchant vessels
were sailing behind Van Tromp's war-ships. Blake
attacked as soon as he could get within firing distance. The tiny squadron of English ships was
soon surrounded by the overpowering numbers of the
Dutch, but they fought as English sailors can when
the fever of battle is upon them. The English ships
were shattered from rigging to hull, and on one vessel
alone the captain and a hundred men were slain.
Blake himself was badly wounded in the thigh. At
last night fell, and the desperate battle ceased for a
while. In the darkness of the night both fleets sailed
together towards the Straits of Dover, and on the
following day the English fleet was reinforced, and
the battle was resumed. The English tried to pierce
through the line of the Dutch men-of-war in order
to reach the merchant ships, which were hurrying
before the wind towards the French coast. Through
the whole of Saturday and the following Sunday the
wonderful and terrible battle continued. The English
were slowly winning, and several Dutch war-ships had
been sunk or captured. At last a part of the English
fleet broke through the Dutch line of battle and
captured fifty merchant vessels. Their success was
stopped by the approach of night. The darkness
was utilised by Van Tromp to escape further disaster.
Taking advantage of the tide and wind, he turned
his shattered fleet homewards, and before the morning
broke he was out of reach of the English.

This was Blake's last encounter with the Dutch.
His wound in the thigh prevented him com-

manding for some time, and when he had recovered his strength the Dutch had made their peace with England.

By these series of victories Blake had proved himself to be the greatest English admiral since the days of Drake and Sir Richard Grenville. But no rest did he get even now. England declared war against Spain, and Blake was sent out to imitate Drake's exploits in the West Indies.

THE ATTACK ON SANTA CRUZ.

The last and most famous exploit of Admiral Blake was his attack on the Spaniards at Santa Cruz de Teneriffe. The defence of Taunton and the battles with Van Tromp and De Ruyter had made Blake the hero of his country, but the story of his victory at Santa Cruz was heard with wonder and admiration by the whole of Europe. Even the Spaniards themselves could not withhold their praise of the daring courage and skill of their enemy, while the Royalists, who hated Blake's political opinions, were roused to enthusiasm for the man who had given such a blow to the common enemy of every Englishman.

Santa Cruz is a long and narrow bay in one of the Canary Islands, with an entrance like the neck of a bottle. On each side of this neck strong forts had been built by the Spaniards, and others were placed at intervals all round the shore of the bay. Each fort was armed with heavy cannon, ready to blow any ship out of the water that dared to venture in without the consent of the Spaniards. But besides these defences there was another danger

which an enemy might have to face if he ventured
to attack this stronghold. It happens that the
wind generally blows into the bay from the sea,
or else is very still and calm. In this case if a fleet
entered the bay to attack a Spanish vessel it would
probably be becalmed opposite the enemy's guns,
and would find it difficult to get out again.

In this well-guarded bay sixteen Spanish
treasure-ships had taken refuge, waiting for an
opportunity to slip across to the Spanish coast
when the English fleet was well out of the way.
They never dreamed that Blake, or any other
English seaman, would venture his head down the
bottle-necked bay of Santa Cruz. But they little
knew the man who was in command of England's
fleet. No sooner did Blake hear of the whereabouts of the treasure-ships than he immediately
set sail, and reached the bay on April 20th, 1656.

The wind and tide were favourable, and Blake
immediately gave orders for the fleet to move into
the bay. The Spanish galleons were drawn up in
a line with their broadsides facing the entrance to
the bay. Behind them ten of the smallest ships
were lying in a half circle close to the shore. Blake
saw at a glance that this was a very bad position
for the Spaniards, for the small ships and many of
the forts would be prevented from using their guns
for fear of hitting the galleons. This was what
really happened. Captain Stayner, in command of
one squadron of the English fleet, went boldly
through the entrance of the bay, and turned his
vessels broadside on to the six Spanish galleons.
Blake himself concentrated his fire on the shore

batteries. For four hours the six treasure ships bore the brunt of the battle, while the ten small vessels and many of the batteries on shore remained silent, with their gunners idle, watching the volumes of smoke rolling across the bay, and hearing the thunder of the battle in which they could take no part. At last the firing ceased, and the smoke was wafted away. Then the Spaniards on shore and in the small vessels perceived that every one of the six great galleons had surrendered to the English. But the battle was not yet over. In fact, Blake's fleet was in more danger now, because the shore batteries and the small vessels could at length open fire without the fear of hitting their comrades. The six large galleons were now manned by English crews, who would suffer severely directly the land batteries opened fire. Blake instantly saw this danger, and promptly proceeded to avert it. He gave orders for his men to withdraw from the captured ships, and to set them on fire. In a short time these orders were carried out, and while the great galleons blazed in fierce flames, the English fleet closed upon the ten small ships, and set them on fire also. Now the wind which had carried the English fleet into the bay shifted in a manner which seemed miraculous to the superstitious sailors. No sooner had they finished their terrible work of destruction among the Spanish vessels than the wind blew steadily from the shore, and carried them out of the bay beyond the fire of the Spanish batteries. With this favourable wind they sped swiftly back to Cadiz, leaving behind them the blazing and shattered galleons.

K

The news of this victory was received in England with wild enthusiasm. Lord Clarendon himself was only stating the common opinion of his countrymen when he wrote the following words:—

"The whole action was so miraculous that all men who knew the place wondered that any sober men, with what courage soever endued, would ever have undertaken it; and they could hardly persuade themselves to believe what they had done, whilst the Spaniards comforted themselves with the belief that they were devils and not men who had destroyed them in such a manner."

Not long after this achievement Blake broke down in health. For more than a year he had been on board ship without having landed once, and the close confinement and lack of fresh food and vegetables had had their usual effect. He was attacked with the scurvy, and his constitution, which had been weakened by wounds, could not resist this disease. When his ships were at last ordered home he knew that he was dying. He uttered a wish that he might live long enough to step for the last time upon his native shore; but two hours before his ship, the *George*, sailed into Plymouth Sound, in the year 1657, the great admiral died.

VII.

LORD CLIVE

AND

THE INDIAN EMPIRE.

Since 1875 the sovereign of this country has borne the splendid title of "Queen of Great Britain and Ireland and Empress of India." A glance at a geography book tells us that the Indian Empire is twenty-seven times as large as England, and eleven times as large as the whole of the United Kingdom. In this vast country two hundred and eighty-six millions of people live under British rule, or, in other words, one-sixth of the whole population of the world.

Great Britain owes this great and splendid empire to one man, above all, named Robert Clive, who went out to India about a century and a half ago, in the humble capacity of a clerk in the office of a company of merchants.

Robert Clive was born at Market Drayton, in Shropshire. He was sent to school at an exceptionally early age, and gave his masters more trouble than even most English schoolboys. He had a fiery temper and a daring courage, and he was always more ready to give one of his comrades a black eye or a broken pate than to hand a neatly written lesson to his master. One day he terrified the inhabitants of Market Drayton by climbing to the top of the church tower and dangling his legs over a water-spout. He also played many wild and mischievous pranks, so that it is not surprising that his parents should have looked upon him as a ne'er do-well. When he was seventeen they were

LORD CLIVE.

(From the Portrait by Gainsborough.)

glad to accept a clerkship for him in the Honourable East India Company, and sent him to Madras, where they would no longer be troubled by his turbulent behaviour.

The East India Company was a company of merchants trading chiefly with India, but also with

China, and other parts of the East. They had established settlements, or "factories," as they were called, at Bombay, Madras, Calcutta, and other places, and already, when Clive first joined the company, they had built up an enormous trade. The responsibilities and power of the company lay in the hands of the directors. These directors acquired very great fortunes and lived in a state of great splendour and magnificence. But in spite of this wealth they paid miserable salaries to the clerks and junior officials in the employment of the company, so that, in order to maintain themselves, the latter were obliged to trade on their own account with the natives of India.

It was to the settlement of Madras, in the part of India called the Carnatic, that Clive proceeded in 1744 as a junior clerk in the service of the Honourable East India Company.

Clive had not been long in India before war broke out between Great Britain and France. The East India Company soon realised that the war would prove a serious trouble to them. The French had also established trading settlements in India, and at this time they were playing a very important part, owing to the ambition and genius of a great Frenchman named Dupleix.

This man was the first person to realise that a small body of well-trained European soldiers was a match for ten times their number of the native soldiers of India. He also proved that the natives themselves might be trained in the European methods of warfare, and that when they acquired this discipline they made brave and reliable soldiers. When Dupleix had proved these facts to his satisfaction, he proceeded to use them to advance the interests and power of his nation in India. The native sovereigns and princes of India were continually at war with one another. The secret ambition of Dupleix was to found a French empire in India, and he resolved to profit by this rivalry of the native rulers.

An excellent opportunity soon presented itself for his schemes. A pretender named Mirzapha Jung claimed the government belonging to the Viceroy of the Deccan. Another pretender, named Chunda Sahib, claimed to be the rightful Nabob, or ruler, of the Carnatic instead of the one then in power. Dupleix was in command of a small French army and a large force of well-trained Sepoys, and he determined to support the cause of the pretenders. He had no doubt that if he placed them on the thrones which they coveted, they would be so dependent upon him that he would be the real ruler of a large part of India.

This plan succeeded admirably for the French. Dupleix joined forces with the two pretenders, and waged warfare against the Viceroy of the Deccan and the Nabob of the Carnatic. The French soldiers were found to be irresistible against the native armies, and Dupleix soon seated the two pretenders upon the thrones of the Deccan and the Carnatic. Dupleix himself was all-powerful, and he maintained a state of great magnificence and pomp. The natives of India regarded the French with profound respect, and the ambitious dreams of Dupleix seemed likely to be realised.

When, therefore, war broke out between Great

Britain and France Dupleix instantly resolved to
drive out the British, w. · were likely to hinder
his schemes of a French empire in India. The
armies of the two pretenders were at his disposal,
and with these he hoped to crush the British before
they were joined by the native princes who sided
against the French.

The first attack of the French was upon Madras,
which was one of the largest stations of the East
India Company in the province called the Carnatic.
A French fleet appeared before the town, and it was
soon obliged to surrender.

Clive himself escaped from the town in the dis-
guise of a Mussulman, and sought refuge at Fort
St. David, near Madras, where there was a small
garrison of soldiers in the service of the East India
Company.

The British garrison at Fort St. David had a
few skirmishes with the French and their native
allies, in which Clive distinguished himself by his
bravery. He now entered the army in the service
of the East India Company, with the rank of ensign,
and was soon promoted to a captaincy.

The French were now besieging the town of
Trichinopoly. Upon the garrison of this town
depended the fortune of the East India Company.
If Trichinopoly fell, the Indian Empire would be in
the hands of the French and their allies.

Clive himself had carried supplies into the town
through the besieging force, and had come back
with the report that the garrison was disheartened
and on the point of surrender. He saw clearly that
there was only one means by which the French

successes could be checked. He proposed to the governor of Fort St. David that an attack should be made upon the town of Arcot, which was the capital of the Carnatic and the favourite residence of the Nabobs. This would probably have the effect of withdrawing the enemy from the walls of Trichinopoly. The Governor of Fort St. David was immediately struck in favour of this plan. He withdrew nearly the whole garrison from Madras to Fort St. David, and gave to Clive himself the honour of commanding this force.

THE GALLANT DEFENCE OF ARCOT.

With a small army of two hundred Europeans and three hundred Sepoys, or native soldiers, Clive set out on that expedition which was to bring him a lasting fame. A terrific thunderstorm raged over their heads, but Clive led his little army onwards steadily and rapidly towards Arcot. The native soldiers were deeply impressed by the strict discipline which Clive maintained, and they caught his spirit of enthusiasm. At the end of six days they arrived at the town of Arcot. At the sight of this little army a panic seized the eleven hundred native soldiers who formed the garrison, and they fled without firing a shot. Then Clive entered the town at the head of his soldiers, and as they passed on their way to the fort the streets were lined with thousands of natives, who gazed at the victorious army with wonder and awe.

Clive was fully aware that as soon as the native soldiers had recovered from their panic and learnt the smallness of the British force, they would try to regain the town. He also hoped that as soon as the besiegers of Trichinopoly heard of the capture of Arcot they would send some of their forces to attack him. He therefore made every preparation for a vigorous defence.

Things turned out as he had expected. The

CLIVE AT ARCOT.

panic-stricken garrison returned at the end of a few days and surrounded the town.

Clive was not the sort of man to sit down quietly while the enemy fired their guns over the wall. Twice he sallied out of the town and, after killing a great number of the enemy, sent them flying helter skelter.

In the meantime Chunda Sahib, whom Dupleix had made Nabob of the Carnatic, learnt the news about Arcot while he was besieging Trichinopoly. Burning with rage at the success of the British, he sent his son Rezza Sahib with an army of four thousand men from Trichinopoly to regain the chief town of the Carnatic.

Rezza Sahib marched rapidly to Arcot, and on his way he was joined by one hundred and fifty French soldiers, each of whom was worth, in fighting value, six natives. With this army he entered the city of Arcot and took up his position in the Nabob's palace.

Clive sallied out once more and drove back the French, but he was at last compelled to return to the fort after losing many of his men. Three days afterwards Rezza Sahib was joined by another two thousand men.

Now followed one of the most remarkable sieges in the history of the British Empire. The fort in which Clive was stationed was situated in the centre of the town. It was more than a mile round the walls, but it was in a state of great dilapidation. The walls were crumbling, the towers at each corner of the fort were in ruins, and the moat was dry in many places and choked with rubbish. This was the tumbledown place which Clive was bold enough to defend with two hundred Englishmen and three hundred Sepoys against an enemy of twenty times that number.

For fifty days and nights a ceaseless din of musketry and a roar of shot and shell raged round the fort. Day after day Clive made a tour of the ramparts to see that every man was in his place and he animated his soldiers with cheerful speeches and an example of perfect courage, energy and vigilance. He ordered a mound to be made inside the fort, from which his gunners could fire upon the Nabob's palace, and he commanded barriers of earth to be thrown up inside the walls, so that when a breach was made by the enemy they would find another obstacle to encounter.

By degrees the food supply within the fort became very scanty, and at last even the rice began to fail. Clive feared that his men, especially the native soldiers, might become rebellious under the pangs of hunger. But he was mistaken. The Sepoys came to their chief, whom they had learnt to love as a hero, but it was not to complain of their short commons. They begged that all the grain should be reserved for the Europeans, who needed more nourishment than the natives, and they said that the water in which the rice had been boiled would suffice for themselves. There is hardly any incident in history which is such a noble example of self-devotion as this story of the Sepoys who served under Robert Clive.

At last Clive sent entreaties for assistance to the chief of a wild tribe of native warriors, called Mahrattas, who were always willing to hire themselves out to fight for any general who paid them generously, and who seemed to be on the winning side. Rezza Sahib learnt that the Mahrattas were preparing to assist the English, and he decided to make a determined attack upon the fort before the Mahrattas arrived upon the scene. The day chosen for this attempt was a great festival with the Mahommedans. On these occasions they used to work themselves up

to a state of religious frenzy, and drank an intoxicating liquor named *bang* which made them half
mad, and as furious as wild beasts.

Clive was warned by his spies that this attack
was to be made. After making every preparation
for defence he lay down to sleep, worn out with his
exertions and anxiety. At break of day the enemy
rushed furiously to the attack, wild with enthusiasm
and intoxicating *bang*. They attempted to batter
down the gates by means of elephants with iron
plates on their heads, but the monsters were wounded
and terrified by the English musketry, and they
turned round and charged their own masters, throwing them into disorder. Then thousands of the
native soldiers waded across the ditch round the fort,
and struggled to enter the breaches in the walls.
Clive's men had been waiting for this, and reserving
their powder and . As soon as the surging crowd
of natives reached the breaches, a storm of shells and
shot was hurled down upon them from the top of the
walls, while the cannon were fired with steady volleys
into the midst of the advancing army. After long
and desperate assaults the enemy was beaten back at
all points with heavy loss. At last the firing ceased,
and in the darkness of night Rezza Sahib retreated
hurriedly from Arcot, leaving behind him guns,
ammunition, and his treasure chest. When morning
broke Clive saw that he had gained the victory. He
marched out to survey the camp with the two
hundred soldiers who were all that survived the
dreadful siege, and who had gained the deathless
honour of keeping at bay ten thousand soldiers for
seven weeks.

Clive now entered upon a series of victories which destroyed the French power in India and established the reputation of the British arms.

The East India Company looked upon Clive as the only man who could maintain their position against the French and the usurper, Chunda Sahib, who were striving to drive the English out of India. They gave Clive the chief command of their forces. Two hundred British soldiers and seven hundred Sepoys were sent to him, and with these he joined the Mahrattas, and attacked Rezza Sahib at the head of five thousand natives and three hundred Frenchmen. A fierce conflict took place, but Clive's genius and enthusiasm won the day, and Rezza Sahib was utterly defeated. Six hundred native soldiers, trained in European discipline by Dupleix, passed over from the enemy and enrolled themselves in the British force.

Shortly afterwards, with a force of thirteen hundred Sepoys and two hundred and eighty Europeans, Clive attacked and put to flight a force of two thousand Sepoys and four hundred Frenchmen.

After many other encounters with the enemy, in which he greatly distinguished himself, Clive's health broke up, and he was compelled to take a rest from active duty. In 1753 he married a Miss Margaret Maskelyne. This lady, who was distinguished for her charm of manner and numerous accomplishments, made him a good and faithful wife, and he was always devotedly attached to her. Soon after his marriage he returned to England, where he received an enthusiastic welcome.

While Clive was in England great changes took

place in India. The British finally crushed the power of the French, and Dupleix, the great Frenchman who had nearly obtained an Indian empire for his countrymen, returned to Paris, where he died in poverty and disgrace.

THE WAR WITH SURAJAH DOWLAH.

But another enemy had now arisen against the British. The East India Company had established a town and factory at Calcutta, in the province of Bengal. This province was ruled over by a young prince named Surajah Dowlah. This young man had been spoiled and pampered from his childhood. He had never known his will to be thwarted, and as he had never been taught to restrain his evil passions, he had grown up with every vice that it is possible to think of in the human character. Although he was as fickle as a weathercock in most things, he had one idea which never changed. This was a hatred for the English. Shortly after he ascended the throne of the great province of Bengal, he threatened that he would drive every Englishman in Calcutta into the sea. On the 4th of June, 1756, he advanced towards Calcutta with a large army. The town was defended by a fortification called Fort William, but it was not strong enough to resist a powerful enemy, and the whole garrison was captured. Then one hundred and forty-six prisoners, among whom was one woman, were dragged to the place which has gained an awful fame under the name of the "Black Hole of Calcutta." It was a small chamber hardly large enough for six people, and into this den those one hundred and forty-six miserable human beings were thrust by the spear heads of Surajah Dowlah's brutal soldiers. A night of sickening horror followed In the morning twenty-five out of one hundred and forty-six were all that survived, and when they were led out of the den not a mother would have recognised her son, so much had they altered during that night of horror.

The news of this tragedy at Calcutta reached Madras on August 16th. Clive immediately volunteered to lead a force to Bengal to give a proper punishment to Surajah Dowlah. But there were many officers of the East India Company who were jealous of Clive's position, and it took two months of disputing before he was given the command. At last, with nine hundred European soldiers and twelve hundred Sepoys, Clive set sail from Madras to Calcutta.

Several severe fights took place with the enemy, and some months later Calcutta surrendered to the English, and it was taken possession of in the name of the British Government.

A correspondence now took place between Clive and Surajah Dowlah. The latter was never of the same opinion for two days together. On one occasion he would offer to restore the East India Company's property and to give them compensation for their losses, and shortly afterwards he would threaten to kill every Englishman in India. If Clive had been allowed to act without hindrance he would probably have crushed this fickle tyrant without loss of time, but he was surrounded by officers who were jealous of his power and who disputed his commands, so that no definite plan was determined upon.

At last he resolved to attack Surajah Dowlah, who was encamped between the British camp and Calcutta. Clive was in command of fourteen hundred Europeans and seven hundred Sepoys, with seven field guns. The Nabob opposed him with forty thousand men, including eighteen thousand cavalry and forty guns.

At six o'clock in the morning Clive ordered the first columns of his army to advance to the attack. A heavy fog shrouded them in darkness, but with a firm and steady front they marched onwards and beat back the advanced guard of the enemy. Presently the fog cleared a little, and Clive perceived a long line of horsemen sweeping down upon them. With perfect discipline the British soldiers halted and formed in squares. Then, as soon as the horsemen came within range, they opened a steady fire upon them. A fearful destruction was made in the ranks of the enemy's cavalry, and before they reached the British squares they wheeled round and retreated at full speed. If the fog had now cleared off, Clive would have inflicted a crushing defeat on Surajah Dowlah. As it was, however, the fog became denser than ever, and the first columns of the British army lost their way and came under the fire of their own comrades.

The British were now surrounded by the Nabob's hordes of warriors, who attacked them in front and rear. They were in a dangerous position, but Clive fired his soldiers with enthusiasm by his presence of mind and amazing courage. With wonderful skill and energy he rallied his men, cut his way through the enemy and reached the shelter of Calcutta,

He had suffered severe losses, but Surajah Dowlah was terrified at the way in which the little British force had cut up his own great army. He sent messages desiring peace. Clive would willingly have punished him once and for all by an overwhelming defeat, but he was afraid that the Nabob might be reinforced by a French army. At length he decided to accept Surajah Dowlah's offers, and a treaty was drawn up and signed by the Nabob, in which he bound himself to restore the factories to the East India Company, to compensate them for their losses by the war, and to give them facilities for free trade throughout his dominion

For a time Surajah Dowlah observed this treaty, but Clive knew quite well that he was only waiting for an opportunity to revenge himself. The Nabob promised assistance to the French if they would attack the English, and offered an enormous sum of money to his principal minister, Meer Jaffier, if he succeeded in destroying them. He was not aware, however, that the officers of his own household were beginning to hate him as much, or more, than they hated the English. His habits, cowardice, and cruelty disgusted even men who had been accustomed to the tyranny of Nabobs. Clive learnt through his spies that Meer Jaffier and the other ministers of Surajah Dowlah were on the point of rebelling against their master. Clive at once came to the conclusion that if he helped to dethrone Surajah Dowlah and placed Meer Jaffier on the throne, he would gain immense power in India. With this purpose in view he entered into secret negotiations with Meer Jaffier and his comrades,

L

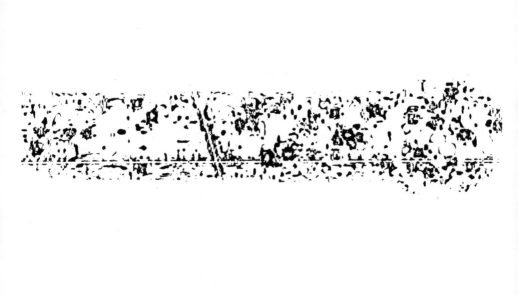

MICROCOPY RESOLUTION TEST CHART

(ANSI and ISO TEST CHART No. 2)

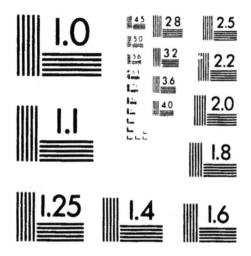

APPLIED IMAGE Inc

1 Main Street
New York   14609   USA
00 – Phone
5989 – Fax

and promised them assistance in dethroning the tyrant.

Meer Jaffier accepted Clive's proposals, and preparations for the plot were secretly carried on. For a time Clive succeeded in deceiving the Nabob with a seeming friendship, but at last Surajah Dowlah's suspicions were aroused. It came to his knowledge that Meer Jaffier was ready to betray him into the hands of the English. He surrounded his minister's house with troops, and, with more energy than usual, prepared for war. Meer Jaffier sent urgent messages to Clive to attack at once. For a long time Clive had been waiting for the proper time to strike his great blow at Surajah Dowlah, and he now gave orders to advance.

It had been arranged that Meer Jaffier was to meet Clive with as large an army as he could induce to fight against the Nabob, but at the last moment his heart failed him and he tried to disarm Surajah Dowlah's suspicions by protesting his fidelity. The Nabob was now fully convinced that Meer Jaffier was a traitor in league with the English, but he was so terrified that he pretended to believe his minister's false assurances of friendship.

THE BATTLE OF PLASSEY.

In the meanwhile Clive was advancing rapidly with his army. The monsoon had set in, and they had to march through a torrent of rain. They trudged through thick mud, and several times they had to wade through water up to their waists, so that it was difficult to keep their ammunition dry. After a weary march they reached Plassey, and

Clive halted in front of a mango grove outside the village. As the army was taking up its position the sounds of military music was borne upon the breeze. It was a warning that the enemy was close at hand.

Sentries were posted, and while his men tried to get some sleep upon the wet ground Clive passed the night thinking out the arrangements for the morrow's battle. The English camp was surrounded by a mud bank and ditch, and Clive had fixed his headquarters in a hunting-lodge which stood at a distance of fifty yards from the bank. On the morning of the following day, June 23rd, 1757, a date which is ever memorable in English history, Clive climbed to the top of the hunting-lodge to obtain a view of the enemy's position.

Surajah Dowlah's army lay stretched out about a mile away. It consisted of thirty-five thousand infantry, fifteen thousand cavalry, and fifty-three heavy guns, besides a small force of French soldiers. As the morning broke they advanced in a long line, and the sun glittered upon their waving banners and flashed from the drawn swords of the cavalry, while the gorgeous costumes of the Nabob's officers and the scarlet trappings of the elephants made a blaze of brilliant colour.

Clive himself was about to attack this great army with only eleven hundred Europeans and two thousand Sepoys. The numbers were, indeed, trivial compared with those of Surajah Dowlah, but Clive had confidence in the courage and fidelity of his own men, whereas the Nabob was trembling every minute lest his soldiers should betray him.

The battle began with a hot fire from the French gunners. Clive was obliged to order his men to take shelter in the mango grove. This was an excellent position of defence, for the men were well protected from the French guns, while they were able to take a well-directed aim at the enemy. For three hours the cannonade lasted, and Clive was now anxiously expecting Meer Jaffier to come to his assistance, but the traitor still hesitated to declare himself openly for the British until they had gained a decided advantage. At mid-day a heavy storm of rain fell, and the Nabob's cavalry now advanced towards the grove, hoping that the British fire was nearly exhausted. Meer Mudan, the gallant leader of the cavalry, charged at the head of his warriors, but they were received by a hail of shot from the British guns, which drove them back. Meer Mudan himself was killed and the enemy was now dis-heartened. Meer Jaffier considered that he might now safely desert the Nabob, and he, at the head of a body of soldiers, moved towards the British army. For a time, however, the British guns kept him at a distance, as Clive's officers did not under-stand that it was Meer Jaffier and a body of deserters.

The French gunners, who had occupied an impor-tant position in advance of Surajah Dowlah's main army, were now compelled to retire. Clive then stationed his artillery nearer the enemy's lines, and ordered them to disable the enemy's guns. Surajah Dowlah's gunners struggled to bring their cannon into action, but man after man fell before the steady fire of the British. At last Clive saw that the moment had arrived to turn the tide of battle. He ordered

CLIVE RECEIVING MEER JAFFIER AT PLASSEY

a general advance of his army. With terrific cheers the British dashed forward. The enemy wavered before the fierce onslaught, and then staggered, broke into disordered masses, and fled in wild retreat. The battle of Plassey was won. With the loss of only twenty-three killed and forty-nine wounded, Clive had gained a victory which would result in bringing the vast and splendid Empire of India under British rule.

Surajah Dowlah fled to Patna, but he was betrayed into the hands of his enemies, and, without Clive's knowledge, was put to death.

Upon the day following the battle, Meer Jaffier paid a visit to Clive, but he was very nervous as to the reception he was likely to receive. Indeed, when a guard of honour turned out to salute him, Meer Jaffier was seen to start violently. He was evidently afraid that Clive's soldiers might have received orders to arrest or shoot him. His fears, however, were groundless, for Clive received him cordially and did not utter a reproach about his double dealings on the previous day. On the contrary, he appointed him as Nabob of the three provinces—Bengal, Behar, and Orissa—and urged him to proceed to Moorshedabad in order to receive the submission of the native officers. A few days later Clive followed the successful traitor to Moorshedabad, and seated him on the throne in the presence of the chief men of the province.

THE BRITISH SUPREMACY IN INDIA.

Clive now became all-powerful in India. Meer Jaffier, the new Nabob, had expected to rule in the same independent way as Surajah Dowlah and his ancestors, but he soon found to his profound dismay that he was playing "second fiddle" to Clive. The only way in which he could retain his position was by keeping on good terms with the British, and to do this he was obliged to give them unlimited privileges of trade and new lands. Clive's schemes had been perfectly successful. He had placed a man on the throne of Bengal who was merely his instrument and could act in no way without his authority. The natives were deeply impressed with the power of the British, and paid supreme homage to Clive. The East India Company became immensely powerful and wealthy, and the whole trade of India now passed through their hands.

Clive was appointed Governor of Bengal, and he exercised his power in such a way that he proved himself to be as great a statesman as he was daring in war. He had enormous difficulties to overcome, but he met them with a masterly courage and power. The French were still at war with the British, and made strenuous efforts to regain their former power in India. At this time also Great Britain was at war with Holland, and a Dutch fleet sailed into Madras harbour to attack the East India Company. Meer Jaffier, who was a born traitor, and could not be loyal even to the man who had placed him on the throne, secretly encouraged the French and Dutch against the British.

To add to Clive's difficulties, a native prince, called the Shahzada, claimed the throne of Bengal, Behar, and Orissa. He gathered together a great army, and attacked Meer Jaffier and the British.

Clive, by prudent statesmanship and unflinchir courage, overcame all these obstacles to Bri h supremacy in India. The French and Dutch were driven out of India, and the Shahzada's army was destroyed. From Calcutta to Madras the British were now triumphant, and the wealth of the Indian Empire poured into the coffers of the East India Company.

THE REFORMATION OF THE EAST INDIA COMPANY.

Clive at length returned to England, where he was received with acclamation by the whole nation. He entered Parliament, and gave valuable advice to the Government with regard to the proper control of affairs in India.

Unfortunately, during his absence from India the state of things in that country became most unsatisfactory. We have already said that the East India Company paid miserable salaries to its junior officials, and they were, therefore, obliged to increase their incomes by trading on their own account. When the Company became all-powerful in India, through the genius of Clive, this practice of private trade was abused to an abominable extent. The junior officials, taking advantage of the power of the Company, grasped the natives' money and oppressed them to such a degree that they had even been more prosperous under the tyranny of such rulers as Surajah Dowlah. The natives were fast learning to hate the name of Englishman with an intense bitterness, and all the influence which Clive had gained by his strict justice and humanity was destroyed by these greedy officials.

At last matters became so bad that Clive was again sent out to India to do away with these abuses. He was once more appointed Governor and Commander-in-Chief of Bengal. No sooner had he set foot in India than, with his usual energy and courage, he set to work to bring about a reformation in the Company. One of his first reforms was to forbid the Company's officers to trade on their own account. Although he compensated them somewhat for their loss by raising their salaries, this new rule caused bitter opposition. Clive was hated by every member of the Company who had grown rich by oppressing the natives.

Clive now gained a victory more difficult even than that of Plassey. A number of British officers in command of the native regiments belonging to the Company, indignant at the reforms which Clive was enforcing, mutinied against him, and sent in their resignations. It was a difficult and dangerous position. Only a few officers remained faithful to the Governor, but Clive acted with a courage and determination which deserve the highest praise.

He was resolved to restore order at any price. "I must see the soldiers' bayonets levelled at my throat," he said, "before I can be induced to give way." He placed the leaders of the rebellion under arrest, and sent them to England. The others he sent down to Calcutta, and replaced them by good non-commissioned officers and soldiers on whom he could rely. Then he pointed out to the rebellious officers that disobedience is one of the worst crimes that a soldier can commit. He showed them the consequences of their act. If they mutinied against their Commander-in-Chief, the native soldiers would be encouraged to rebel against the officers themselves, and a terrible state of affairs might result. Clive's vigorous conduct was successful. The officers were brought back to a sense of their duty, and those who had resigned petitioned to be restored to their positions. Clive now acted with as great a moderation as he had formerly been resolute. He accepted the officers' apologies, and gave them back their rank. The danger was now at an end, and from that day to this our British officers have always been loyal to their country and faithful to their duty.

Many other abuses were put down by Clive's strong hand, and when he returned to England in 1767, he had restored order and good government to the East India Company.

Unfortunately, Clive's strict and vigorous actions raised up a host of enemies against him, and he had no sooner set foot in England than they tried to disgrace him in the eyes of his countrymen. Abominable stories were circulated which accused him of having committed every possible crime in India. At last he was called upon by Parliament to defend his conduct in India before a Committee of the House of Commons.

He was put upon his defence "more," as he said, "like a sheep stealer than a member of the House of Commons." One of the chief accusations against him was that he had committed a crime when he accepted a sum of £200,000 from Meer Jaffier as a reward for having placed him upon the throne.

There is no need here to discuss at length how far Clive was wrong in this matter. There can be no doubt that nowadays a general would have no right to accept any sum of money from a foreign prince for services rendered in warfare. There was a difference, however, in Clive's case. In the first place, he was a servant of the East India Company, and not appointed directly by the British Government. Secondly, it was the national custom of Indian princes to make rich presents to those who had served them.

Clive made a long and eloquent speech in his own defence. When he came to this last accusation, he broke out with indignant words:

"When I recollect entering the Nabob's treasury at Moorshedabad, with heaps of gold and silver to the right and to the left, and these crowned with jewels, by Heavens! at this moment do I stand astonished at my own moderation!"

Clive's defence made it clear that his conduct in India had been entirely in the interest of his country, and that he deserved the gratitude of his countrymen for all time.

The House of Commons acquitted him of any crime, and a resolution was passed unanimously that "Robert, Lord Clive, did render great and meritorious services to his country."

Clive's reputation was now cleared, and the English nation looked upon him once more as a great hero. But, although his enemies had failed in their efforts to ruin him, they had broken the heart of the greatest Englishman of that time. During his examination in the House of Commons he had been treated in a cruel and ignoble manner. He was conscious that he had devoted himself entirely to the service of his country, which had dealt with him in return like a common malefactor. It was more than his proud spirit could bear, and when the excitement of the enquiry was over, he settled into a gloomy and dejected mood which no effort on the part of his friends could remove. His mind was unhinged, and, at last, at the early age of forty-nine, this great Englishman, whose name now shines with a splendid fame which no one can deny him, put an end to his life with his own hand.

The East India Company survived his death for nearly a century, but gradually its powers were taken over by the British Government, and, at last, after the great Indian Mutiny in 1857, it ceased to exist, and Queen Victoria became sovereign of India, and was proclaimed Empress in 1875.

VIII.

GENERAL WOLFE

THE DOMINION OF CANADA.

A CITIZEN of the United Kingdom visiting for the
first time the Canadian province of Quebec, can hardly
believe that he is in a British country. He meets
thousands of people who speak French as their native
language, and who practise many customs which they
seem to have learnt from the peasants of Normandy
and Brittany. In their churches the Roman Catholic
religion is taught, and in their Courts of Justice
many French laws are administered. The same
customs and the same language are to be found in
the Maritime Provinces of Canada. Indeed, throughout the great Dominion, little colonies of people may
be found speaking the language and retaining the
old customs of France.

How is it, one may ask, that so many French
people dwell in a British country under British rule?

The answer to this question is to be found in the
life of James Wolfe, for it was this great general,
aided by gallant British soldiers, who conquered
Canada from the French rulers to whom it first
belonged, and who added the wealth and greatness
of the Dominion to the British Empire.

James Wolfe was born in 1727, at Westerham,

JAMES WOLFE.

in Kent. He was the son of a distinguished soldier, General Edward Wolfe, and of a beautiful and accomplished lady, named Henrietta Thompson.

From a very early age he longed to become a soldier like his father, and when he was fifteen years old he entered the army of King George II. with the rank of ensign. He soon showed an extraordinary capacity for commanding men and inspiring them with his own enthusiasm. There was plenty of fighting to be done in those days, for England was at war with her old enemy, France. Then, in 1745, Bonnie Prince Charlie crossed over the Scottish Border with his Highlanders, and proclaimed himself king in defiance of King George. Wolfe, the boy soldier, commanded a regiment of foot against the French at the Battle of Dettingen, and afterwards took part in the Battle of Culloden Moor, when Prince Charlie's Highlanders were utterly defeated, and the brave but rash young prince had to fly for his life.

At the early age of twenty-three Wolfe obtained the rank of lieutenant-colonel, and he commanded his regiments in the wild districts of Scotland. He afterwards took part in an expedition against the French port of Rochefort. This was a disastrous failure. Most of the English officers who commanded the expedition were severely blamed for their mismanagement. Wolfe, however, was excepted from the general blame. His fellow-officers acknowledged that if his advice had been followed, the failure of the expedition would never have occurred. His conduct on this occasion attracted the notice of William Pitt, the great English statesman who afterwards became the Earl of Chatham.

At this time Pitt's great ambition was to strike a blow at France, then at war with England, by attacking her Canadian colonies. This was a perilous undertaking. The principal towns of Canada—Quebec, Montreal, and Louisburg—were strongly fortified and defended by some of the best troops and the most distinguished generals of France. Then, the climate of Canada is so severe that for many months in the year the seas and rivers are ice-bound. Again, the country was such an enormous distance from any British port that if British sailors or soldiers were once landed on the coast, they might starve before supplies could be sent to them from England. Yet in spite of all these difficulties, Pitt determined to send out a British army to attack Canada.

THE SIEGE OF LOUISBURG.

In June, 1758, Admiral Boscawen, with a splendid fleet of English battleships carrying on board eleven thousand six hundred soldiers, sailed outside the harbour of Louisburg on the rocky shore of Cape Breton. The town of Louisburg was strongly fortified, and defended by a garrison of French soldiers numbering three thousand and eighty, with a force of armed citizens and a band of Indians. On the walls of the fortifications were two hundred and forty cannon, and in the harbour were twelve battleships containing three thousand men. The French were nearly equal in number and much stronger in position than the English, but in the English army was an officer who was worth a host in himself. This was Colonel Wolfe.

The English captured the ships in the harbour

and surrounded the fortifications of Louisburg. Wolfe was the life and soul of the attack. His tall, thin figure was to be seen in the foremost of the fight, animating his soldiers with fiery words, and dashing in advance when any of his men fell back before the hot fire of the enemy. After a gallant defence on the part of the French, the courage and determination of the English soldiers compelled them to surrender. The French stronghold fell into the hands of the English, and Wolfe returned to England, to be welcomed by his countrymen with the well-earned title of the " Hero of Louisburg."

The man who had gained this title was in no way like the popular idea of a hero in outward appearance. His features were very peculiar, indeed, almost comical. He had a turned-up nose, a receding chin, and a sloping forehead. His legs were long and thin, his chest narrow, and his hair a fiery red. His constitution was very delicate. At sea he was always sick, and on land he was very often an invalid. It seemed difficult to believe that this peculiar-looking young man was in any way heroic. But his soldiers and fellow officers knew that in that feeble frame beat a hero's heart which no danger could affright. He had a burning love for his country, and whenever any service was to be done, or any danger to be encountered in the service of that country, he constrained his poor weak body to execute the commands of his daring and enthusiastic spirit.

Such was the character of the man whom William Pitt, the Prime Minister of England, now selected to undertake a task so difficult and daring that it seemed almost hopeless. This was nothing less than to attack

Quebec, the capital of Canada, and the strongest fortress of the French in their western colonies.

At this time Wolfe was over thirty years old, but Pitt raised him to the rank of major-general, gave him supreme command of the expedition, and allowed him to choose his own officers. Wolfe did not take heed of superiority of rank or age, but he chose those officers on whose courage and talent he could most rely. This way of going to work greatly shocked one of the king's ministers, who told his sovereign that Pitt's new general was mad. "Mad, is he?" cried King George, "then I hope he will bite some others of my generals."

THE SIEGE OF QUEBEC.

On the 17th of February, 1759, the English fleet set sail from Spithead. Wolfe himself was on board the *Neptune* with Admiral Saunders. As usual, the sea made him horribly ill, but he stood on board his vessel and directed the arrangements of his troops, regardless of his pain and sea-sickness. Across the Atlantic sailed the fleet to the harbour of Louisburg, where they were reinforced by another squadron of ships and soldiers. Wolfe was now in command of nearly nine thousand men. He was well satisfied with their condition. "Our troops are good," he wrote to Pitt, "and if valour can make amends for the want of numbers, we shall probably succeed."

On the 6th of June the fleet sailed out of Louisburg harbour, and towards the end of June they reached the river St. Lawrence. On June 26th they anchored off the island of Orleans, which lies

M

in the mouth of the St. Lawrence, a few miles from Quebec. Here Wolfe landed with the army and drove back the inhabitants, who made a feeble attempt to oppose them.

From this island Wolfe gazed across the river to Quebec, and for the first time he realised the difficulty—indeed, almost the impossibility—of his task.

Three or four miles away the city of Quebec was perched upon a great rock which served as a natural fortress. Behind the city itself the cliffs rose higher and steeper to form Cape Diamond. Wolfe, gazing across the water, could see the stone houses clustered on the rock, with here and there the spire of a church, the gabled roof of a convent, or the turrets of a palace or hospital. This lofty stronghold was defended by a great number of batteries. The rocks above bristled with cannon, while below the cliff long lines of these iron monsters guarded the strand, ready to belch forth fire and shot upon any English ship venturesome enough to face them.

Quebec stands on a bold promontory which projects into the river St. Lawrence. On the side nearest to the island of Orleans, where the English army was encamped, the river St. Charles divides it from the low-lying ground which stretches along the banks of the St. Lawrence. It is impossible to understand the siege of Quebec without studying the map, but a glance at this will explain the position of the French and English better than any words. All along the banks of the river as far as the falls of Montmorenci the French had thrown

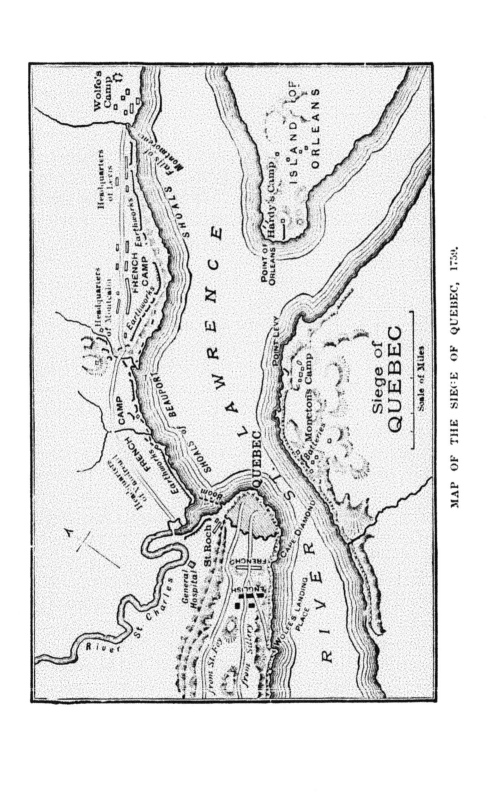

MAP OF THE SIEGE OF QUEBEC, 1759.

up earthworks, behind which stood strong batteries of guns. In the river itself were floating batteries and a number of gunboats and fireships. A thousand sailors manned the gunboats. Fourteen thousand French soldiers and a large body of Indians guarded the shore from Quebec to the falls of Montmorenci, while the city of Quebec itself was defended by nearly two thousand men. Thus it will be seen that the French forces numbered more than sixteen thousand men, with the advantage of a natural stronghold of extraordinary strength, while the British forces commanded by General Wolfe numbered only nine thousand men.

The land forces of the French were under the command of the Marquis of Montcalm, a general of distinguished bravery and skill, who was aided by other officers who had gained a reputation in many hard-fought battles. Unfortunately for the French, the Governor of Quebec, named Vandreuil, who held a superior rank to the Marquis of Montcalm, was a man with no talent for war. He was also bitterly jealous of Montcalm, and, with a mean and un-patriotic spirit, was always more ready to upset Montcalm's plan of action than to co-operate with him loyally against the enemy.

Montcalm himself was always on the alert, and fortified every point which might be attacked by the British.

Never did a British general have to face a more formidable enemy than Wolfe did when he looked across to Quebec from the island of Orleans. Never, also, did a British general face that enemy with more determination and courage.

THE FRENCH FIRE-SHIPS.

Two nights after the British army had landed on the island of Orleans the French made an effort to destroy the English fleet which lay at anchor. It was eleven o'clock and the night was very dark. The British sentries paced up and down the Point of Orleans, straining their eyes through the darkness for any sign of the enemy. Suddenly they became aware of dark masses, blacker even than the shadows of the night, approaching across the water, and they guessed that they were French ships. Suddenly tongues of fire leapt into the darkness and outlined the masts and rigging of the ships. Then a terrific explosion resounded across the sea, followed by another and yet another. The tongues of flame melted into masses of roaring fire, which floated nearer and nearer to the British fleet, threatening it with destruction. It was the French fire-ships, which were being sailed towards the English fleet by a French officer named Delouche. They had been daubed with pitch and tar, and crowded with bombs, old cannon loaded with shot and iron; they were filled with every kind of explosive. Unfortunately for his scheme, Delouche lost his nerve at the last moment and set fire to the vessels before they were near enough to the British fleet. One French captain and half-a-dozen sailors were burnt alive before they could escape in the boats, and many of the fire-ships ran ashore before they reached a British vessel. The others were captured by daring English sailors, who rowed towards them in small boats, grappled them with hooks, towed them to the shore, and then watched them, at a safe distance, exploding, burning, hissing, and crackling with harmless fury.

Soon after this failure on the part of the French, Wolfe sailed from the island of Orleans and captured a promontory on the same side of the river, named Point Levi. This is opposite the city of Quebec, and from this ground Wolfe hurled shot and shell into the town. But it was dreadful and almost useless work, for although he might destroy a multitude of houses it would be just as difficult to capture the city as long as the French army guarded the inaccessible rock upon which it was built.

At last Wolfe grew weary of this continual fighting without result, and he determined to strike a blow full in the face of the French army.

THE ATTACK ON THE BEAUPORT SHORE.

Along the Beauport shore of the St. Lawrence, where the French army was entrenched, the banks of the river were very steep. A mile from Montmorenci, a broad strand lies between the banks of the river and the water, and at low tide a floor of mud nearly half a mile wide joins the dry strand. Upon the edge of the strand the French had erected gun batteries, and these were defended by the guns in the entrenchments which lined the banks above. It was this position which Wolfe decided to attack. He was not aware that the gun batteries on the strand could be aided by the French fire from the entrenchments above. He hoped that if he attacked one of the batteries down below, the French would come down from their entrenchments, and he would thus be able to fight them on equal ground.

Wolfe left sufficient forces to guard Point Levi, and with five thousand men in a fleet of boats he appeared in front of the village of Beauport. This was only to deceive the French. The Marquis of Montcalm was doubtful whether Wolfe intended to force a landing at Beauport or at some other part of the shore, and his perplexity increased when the boats rowed to and fro to hide their real design.

In the meanwhile the British warship *Centurion* anchored near the Falls of Montmorenci and opened fire upon the batteries on the strand. Shortly afterwards two gunboats crept close to the redoubt and fired upon it until the tide went out, leaving them stranded on the mud. Then a battery of forty cannon, which Wolfe had erected on the heights of Montmorenci, fired across the Falls into the French entrenchments. The tide was now out, and t time had come for the great action. Wolfe's fleet of boats rowed steadily towards the French batteries on the strand, and the troops jumped ashore on to the oozy mud left by the receding tide. Now a fearful roar of cannon broke forth. The *Centurion* hurled the deadly contents of all her cannon upon the French batteries, while the gunboats stranded upon the mud opened fire simultaneously. The French batteries replied, and under a hailstorm of shot the British troops assembled on the muddy shore. Thirteen companies of Grenadiers and a detachment of Royal Americans were the first to jump from the boats, while Monckton's Brigade and Fraser's Highlanders landed as speedily as possible. Unfortunately the Grenadiers became wild with a desire to get to close quarters with the enemy, and without orders from their officers they

dashed towards one of the batteries beneath the steep
banks of the river.   They captured this from the
French gunners, but no sooner had they done so than
a torrent of shot and shell poured into their ranks
from the enemy's entrenchments above.   Hundreds
of Grenadiers rolled upon the mud, but their comrades, with loud cheers, tried to scramble up the steep
banks.   The French and Canadian troops, secure in
their entrenchments, answered the British cheers with
shouts of " *Vive le Roi !*" and fired incessant volleys
of shot upon the brave fellows who tried desperately
to gain the heights, and who fell dead and wounded
before the deadly storm.   At this moment it began
to rain in torrents, so that the French could no longer
see the Grenadiers.   The ammunition of both French
and English became wet, and the river banks so
slippery that it was impossible to climb them.   Those
of the Grenadiers who remained alive retreated to the
strand, but they would not acknowledge their defeat,
and, with true British blindness on such occasions,
they maintained that the storm had saved the French
from destruction.

Wolfe, however, saw clearly that it would be madness to make another attack upon such an impregnable
position, and he ordered his troops to retreat.   As they
embarked, the French soldiers, with their Canadian and
Indian allies, yelled derisively at the retreating army,
but the British soldiers waved their hats and dared
them to come down and fight on level ground.

Wolfe was bitterly disappointed, and he sternly
reprimanded the Grenadiers for their rashness.   But
still he would not lose heart, and he now adopted a
new plan.   This was to threaten the French above,

instead of below, the city of Quebec. He ordered
Admiral Holmes to take the fleet up the river past
the French batteries, and twelve hundred troops
under Brigadier Murray embarked on flat-bottomed
boats to accompany him. In spite of the French
batteries the British ships succeeded in gaining the
upper part of the river without much damage.
Brigadier Murray tried to gain a footing above
Quebec, but fifteen hundred French soldiers, under
General Bougainville, succeeded in repulsing him
every time he made the attempt.

The British army was now dismayed by the news
that their well-beloved general was dangerously ill.
Wolfe had, until then, been the life and soul of the
army. With untiring energy and vigilance he had
passed from regiment to regiment and from camp
to camp, encouraging the soldiers and directing his
officers. Now he lay ill and helpless in a farmhouse
at Montmorenci. His body was racked with disease,
and his mind suffered from the disappointment of
his hopes and the apparent impossibility of his task.
At last, to the great joy of the army, his health
improved, and he was able, once more, to direct
the operations of the siege.

He now called a council of his officers and asked
them to suggest a scheme for a final and decisive
attack upon the enemy. After many proposals had
been made, equally daring and difficult to accomplish,
one course of action was decided upon by Wolfe and
his officers. This was a desperate plan. On the north
shore of the St. Lawrence, above the city of Quebec,
Wolfe had noticed through his telescope a narrow
path which ran up the face of the woody precipice

At the top he had seen about a dozen white tents, and he thought that the French might be so confident that no danger need be feared in this quarter that the guard might be small enough to be easily overpowered. This place, which was then called *Anse du Foulon*, or Fuller's Cove, is now known as Wolfe's Cove. It is close to a plateau outside the city of Quebec, called the Plains of Abraham. Wolfe's plan was to send about two hundred men up the steep and narrow path of Fuller's Cove, and, if they succeeded in gaining the heights and overpowering the French guard, he would follow, himself, with the whole army.

THE HEIGHTS OF ABRAHAM.

All preparations were now made to carry out this attempt. Nearly the whole of the British troops were withdrawn from their various positions and assembled on the Point of Orleans and Point Levi, as close to Quebec as possible, while a large number of soldiers embarked on Admiral Holmes's ships, where they were joined by Wolfe himself.

In the meanwhile the French had seen the movements of the British army. They thought with joy that Wolfe had abandoned the siege and was about to return to England with his army. Yet they had learnt something of Wolfe's ardent character, and they fully expected a last desperate attack before he took his departure. The Marquis of Montcalm had taken every precaution for defence. Every opening in the cliffs which a cat would have found difficult to climb was defended with a French guard. Even the Anse du Foulon was not neglected, and a French officer named Captain de Vergor, with a body of colonial troops, had been ordered to take up his position at this point.

At last the day arrived when Wolfe decided to make his great effort. In order to direct the attention of the French in another direction, Admiral Saunders was ordered to make a pretended attack upon the Beauport shore. Accordingly, on the night of September 12th, 1759, the Admiral drew up his fleet close to the Beauport shore, and soon every gun and every musket on board the British vessels roared with shot and shell. The Marquis of Montcalm was thoroughly deceived. Nearly the whole of the French army was concentrated upon the Beauport shore, and while Admiral Saunders's fleet thundered defiance, the French gave little heed to the small British fleet which lay silently at anchor in the river above Quebec.

As soon as Wolfe heard the boom of Admiral Saunders's guns he ordered the boats to be lowered and the troops to embark in them. His commands were speedily carried out, and the boats quietly floated down the tide filled with the excited soldiers who, in a short time, expected to be engaged in deadly fight.

Wolfe himself, in spite of the courage which never failed him in the hour of danger, must have felt his heart beat quicker as he sat in his boat and peered through the darkness of night towards the steep cliffs on the top of which the French army was encamped. Not a sound broke through the deep silence but the gentle lapping of the water against the boats and the subdued conversation of the British soldiers. Presently—perhaps to relieve the strain on his feelings—

Wolfe began to recite in a low voice "An Elegy in a Country Churchyard," by the poet Gray. As he came to the line—

'The paths of glory lead but to the grave,"

the words must have touched his heart very deeply, for it was his firm belief that he would die in the battle about to take place.

The soldiers listened in silence to their well-beloved general as the words came from his lips in the darkness. "Gentlemen," he said quietly when the poem was finished, "I would rather have written those lines than take Quebec."

Presently, as the boats came near to the shore, a sudden shout broke the stillness. It was the challenge of a French sentry.

"Who goes there?"

A Highland officer who could speak French fluently, answered the question by a shout of "France!"

"Of what regiment?" continued the sentry.

"Of the Queen's," answered the Highlander, in French.

The sentry was satisfied, for he knew, as did the English also, that some soldiers of that regiment were expected to accompany some French provision boats down the river. The English boats passed on, and a little while later they reached the Anse du Foulon. The troops now landed quietly, and stood on a strand beneath the steep cliffs, which were covered with bushes and trees. Twenty-four men had volunteered to lead the way up the heights; and while their comrades stood on the strand they scrambled up the narrow pathway, helping themselves up by clinging to the bushes on either side. At last they reached the crest of the cliffs, and they immediately perceived the white tents of the French guard appearing through the darkness. Without a moment's hesitation the twenty-four volunteers dashed upon the sleepy French soldiers. Captain de Vergor was captured as he leapt out of bed, and his soldiers fled without much resistance.

The troops waiting below heard the musket shots and cheering, and they guessed that their comrades had gained a footing on the heights. At the word of command from Wolfe they scrambled hastily up the steep pathway. As soon as all the troops had assembled, they took up their position in the level meadow land called the Plains of Abraham. At the further end of them was the city of Quebec, but it was concealed from the eyes of the British army by a ridge of rising ground. This ridge was suddenly crowded by a body of French soldiers, and at the same time a French gun battery near Quebec opened fire on the English ships lying near the Anse du Foulon.

In the meanwhile the Commander-in-Chief of the French forces, the gallant Marquis of Montcalm, had been anxiously watching the movements of the British fleet under Admiral Saunders, without a suspicion of what was taking place on the Heights of Abraham. His attention was directed to that quarter when the boom of the guns met his ears from the battery above Quebec. He rode at full speed to Quebec, and just as he reached the Governor's house he descried with amazement the red coats and tartan kilts of the British army, drawn up in battle array, two miles away, on the Heights of Abraham.

The troops ordered by Montcalm were a long time before they followed their general, and some did not stir at all, Vandreuil, the Governor of Quebec, with his usual jealousy of Montcalm, hindering many of the troops from rendering him assistance. Nevertheless, thousands of French soldiers poured through the quaint old streets of Quebec, followed by bands of Indians in war paint, and crowds of Canadian volunteers.

As soon as the French troops came upon the scene of action they advanced upon the British army, which waited steadily for the attack. Bands of Indian and Canadian sharpshooters took shelter behind bushes and hillocks, and kept up an incessant fire of musketry upon the British troops, while some field guns, dragged from Quebec, thinned Wolfe's ranks with well-directed shot. The advancing French army, with disordered ranks, composed partly of veteran French soldiers and partly of brave but undisciplined Canadian volunteers, opened fire as soon as they came within range.

The British army advanced a short distance to meet them, without firing. Then they halted, and with a deliberate aim fired a steady volley. This was repeated again and again, until a cloud of smoke rolled between the two armies. When it cleared away the French ranks were shattered, hundreds of dead and dying encumbered the ground, and a panic reigned in the disordered mass of soldiers.

Now Wolfe gave the order to charge. It was greeted with a ringing English cheer and the shrill

yell of the Highlanders. Wolfe himself led the
charge at the head of the Louisburg volunteers. As
he ran, a shot broke his wrist. Without a pause he
wrapped his handkerchief round it and ran on. Then
another shot hit him, but still he ran on at the head
of his men until a third shot found its way into his
breast. He staggered back with his arms up and
then sat on the ground. A young officer and three
soldiers bore him in their arms and carried him to
the rear. They wished to call a surgeon to his aid,
but he would not permit this.

"There's no need," he said feebly. "It's all over
with me." A few moments later one of the soldiers
cried out, "They run; see how they run!" "Who
run?" asked Wolfe, raising himself out of a half-
dazed condition. "The enemy, sir," answered the
young officer. "Egad, they give way everywhere!"
A look of joy passed over Wolfe's face, and with a
great effort he ordered one of the soldiers to carry
a message to an officer directing him to cut off the
French retreat. Then he turned on his side, and as
the young officer leant over him he murmured,
"Now, God be praised, I will die in peace!" With
these words fled the spirit of the brave general whose
victory gave the great Dominion of Canada to the
British Empire.

The French were indeed in full flight. The
Marquis of Montcalm himself was shot through the
body as he was carried towards the town by the panic-
stricken soldiers. Shortly afterwards Quebec surrendered to the British, and although in other parts
of Canada the French made a brave resistance, they
were steadily defeated, until at last, when Montreal

surrendered, the whole of Canada passed into British hands.

At the present day there are no more loyal citizens of the British Empire than the descendants of those French Canadians who fought against Wolfe on the Heights of Abraham, and the vast Dominion of Canada is the home of many thousands of British men and women who have left the old country to earn their living in the West.

IX.

WILLIAM PITT, EARL OF CHATHAM,

AND

ENGLISH STATESMANSHIP.

In the eighteenth century, when William Pitt was the chief minister of England, the British Empire attained a height of prosperity and power which surpassed the splendour of every period of its past history, and made it more feared among nations than the Spanish Empire before the days when its " Invincible Armada " was destroyed by English seamen and by the powers of the heavens. While Pitt was at the head of the Government, Clive won the battle of Plassey and placed the splendid Empire of India under British rule. Wolfe was chosen by Pitt himself to lead that expedition against Quebec which shattered the French power in Canada and gave the great Dominion to the British Crown. While Pitt's great spirit guided the public affairs of his country, British men-of-war gained victories in all parts of the world, which struck terror into the hearts of her enemies while they were bound to confess their admiration and astonishment.

To William Pitt, afterwards Earl of Chatham, a very large share in the honour of this national prosperity is due.

To those who have read of Wolfe's splendid

N

conduct at Louisburg, and his heroic capture of Quebec, the honour of the conquest of Canada may seem to rest entirely with that invalid general who lost his life in his country's service on the Heights of Abraham. And so it is with the other victories

WILLIAM PITT, LORD CHATHAM.

(*From a Painting by R. Brompton.*)

of that period. One is apt to think that the British Empire owed its greatness in the eighteenth century entirely to the bravery and genius of soldiers like General Wolfe, and to sailors like Admiral Boscawen or Admiral Hawke.

Yet one must remember that before British generals or British admirals can gain victories, the ships, the sailors and the soldiers, the guns, the powder and shot, and the innumerable requirements of war must be ready for service, and unless those men who are responsible for all this do their duty honestly and well, no general and no admiral could ever gain a victory.

Then, too, all these requirements cannot be obtained without an enormous sum of money, and that money must come out of the people's pockets. But the people will not part with their money if they do not approve of the war, and so there must be someone in whom the people have confidence, and who can persuade them that the war is right and just, and that to carry it out half-heartedly, or without spending the necessary money, would bring ruin and disgrace upon them.

The men who are chiefly responsible for the government of the country are the members of the Cabinet, or Cabinet Ministers, as they are called. Generally, Parliament is divided into two or more parties. In the days of Pitt the members of one of these parties were called Tories and the others Whigs. Nowadays they are generally known as Unionists and Liberals. When either of these parties is in the majority in the House of Commons, the Cabinet Ministers are chosen from that party, and the country is then governed by either a Unionist or a Liberal Government, as the case may be.

There are generally about sixteen Cabinet Ministers, chief among whom is the Prime Minister, who selects the other members of the Cabinet, such as the Foreign Secretary, the Colonial Secretary, the Secretary for War, the First Lord of the Admiralty, and the Secretary for India.

These ministers direct the most important affairs of State, and the welfare of the country depends largely upon their ability, courage, and patriotism.

Sometimes the British public are carried away by some great enthusiasm, or stirred by some great passion. Perhaps they imagine that some foreign nation has offended them, and they clamour eagerly for war when there is no real need to enter into such a deplorable condition. It is then the duty of the Prime Minister and his colleagues to point out to the nation the folly of their desires. If the ministers are strong and have gained the confidence of the people, they can avert such a national disaster as an unnecessary war: but if they are weak they may yield to the clamour of the people, who learn their folly, too late, by bitter experience.

On the other hand, it may sometimes be necessary to declare war against a foreign nation in order to save the country's honour, to maintain its prosperity, to put down some tyrant, or to defend some downtrodden people. In this case perhaps the citizens of the Empire may be too regardless of their honour, or too reluctant to part with their money for the requirements of an honourable war. It is then necessary for the ministers to rouse the people to a proper sense of their duty, and to awaken in them the spirit of their forefathers, who were ready to risk their lives and to spend their fortunes when the country was in danger or its honour at stake.

When William Pitt was a minister, the nation had implicit confidence in his wisdom and patriotism. He awakened in them such a spirit of enthusiasm for the advancement and prosperity of the Empire, that they were eager to pour out their hard-earned wealth to furnish the requirements for his great schemes.

There can be no doubt that William Pitt was too ready to enter into war, and did not think enough of the horrors and misery attending it, but there is no doubt also that he undertook a war because it was his profound conviction that it was necessary for the honour and safety of his nation. Having entered into a war, the whole force of his great genius was directed to the proper management of it, so that it might bring success and increase the power of his country. Every expedition against the enemy was planned by Pitt (except in India, where Clive was alone responsible), every officer in command of an expedition was selected by him, regardless of rank but on account of the ability which Pitt had discovered in him, while all the vast business relating to war, the raising of money, the recruiting of the army and navy, the equipment of the soldiers and sailors, was superintended by Pitt himself.

"The ardour of his soul," says Lord Macaulay, "had set the whole kingdom on fire. It inflamed every soldier who dragged the cannon up the heights of Quebec, and every sailor who boarded the French ships among the rocks of Brittany. The minister, before he had been long in office, had imparted to the commanders whom he employed his own impetuous, adventurous, and defying character. They, like him, were disposed to risk everything, to think nothing done while anything remained undone, to fail rather than not to attempt."

PITT'S EARLY DAYS.

This great Minister was born in the year 1708. He was educated at Eton and Oxford, and afterwards travelled on the Continent for the sake of his health. From his boyhood he suffered terribly from gout, and during the whole of his career this painful malady afflicted him frequently. From the Continent he returned to obtain the rank of a cornetcy in the Life Guards, and in 1735 he entered Parliament as member for Old Sarum.

At that time Robert Walpole was at the head of the Government. He was a remarkable man, who had the welfare of his country sincerely at heart, but who did not scruple to bribe members of Parliament, or, in other words, to pay them to vote as he wished them. He had also an unbounded greed for power. He loved to rule alone, and as he would not allow anyone to share his authority he chose his fellow ministers rather for their lack of talent than for their possession of it, so that they might act simply under his direction.

In consequence of this the most talented men in Parliament joined the Opposition, as that party opposed to the Ministry of the time is always called. At the head of this party was Frederic, Prince of Wales, who was bitterly opposed to his father, George II. One section of the Opposition was composed of young men who called themselves "the patriots," but whom Walpole contemptuously termed "the boys." William Pitt joined this party at the age of twenty-seven, and he soon made himself prominent by his eloquence and his determined attacks upon Walpole.

For this behaviour Walpole took his revenge by dismissing the eloquent young cornet from the army. Pitt did not lose much by this. The Prince of Wales favoured his cause and gave him a post in his household, and he still continued to denounce the administration of Walpole in speeches of astonishing eloquence and power.

It will be well here to describe what manner of man this was who became one of the greatest statesmen of our country.

If anyone were asked what personal attractions would be most valuable to an orator to captivate the imaginations and hearts of an assembly, he might take Pitt for his model.

When Pitt stood up in Parliament and stretched out his right hand to secure the attention of his audience, a hush of admiration and respect fell upon them. He was of a tall and commanding stature. His forehead was high and of noble proportions, his nose prominent and keen like that of a hawk, his mouth was firm, and his eyes of an exceeding brilliancy which seemed literally to flash with fire when his oratory became impassioned. His gestures were graceful and appropriate, and it is said that if he had been upon the stage he would have been one of the greatest actors the world has seen. But that gift which is most valuable to an orator and most pleasing to an audience, that is to say, a fine voice, he had to a remarkable degree of excellence.

By one who heard his oratory it was said that " his voice was both full and clear; his lowest whisper was distinctly heard; his middle tones were sweet, rich, and beautifully varied: when he elevated his voice to its highest pitch the House was completely filled with the volume of sound."

In 1742 Walpole was driven out of office by his enemies, and Henry Pelham and his brother, the Duke of Newcastle, became the chief ministers. All the men of talent, and also, indeed, all the men of no talent, who had been in the ranks of the Opposition against their common enemy, Walpole, now passed over to the side of the Government, and there was no longer any party which could really be called an Opposition.

The time had now come to reward Pitt for his services to his party. He wished to be made Secretary for War, but, unfortunately for his ambition, he had deeply offended King George by some of his youthful speeches, in which he had criticised the king in unguarded terms. The ministers were unable to obtain the king's consent to their proposal that Pitt should be made Secretary for War, and they had to reward him instead by the less important post of Paymaster of the Forces.

Any minister who held this office only received a small salary, but it was a fact known to everyone that the minister always appropriated a large sum of money for his own personal uses out of the enormous sums which passed through his hands for the payment of the soldiers and sailors. At this period of our country's history many of the ministers responsible for the Government offices did not scruple to help themselves largely to the public money entrusted to them. This dishonourable conduct was indeed so common in every Government department, and it was so openly practised, that the conscience of the nation seemed too perverted to regard this great national evil as a matter for much reproach.

When William Pitt became Paymaster of the Forces he set his colleagues an example of honesty

SIR ROBERT WALPOLE.

to which they were not accustomed. He contented himself with his small salary, and not a penny would he keep of the public money passing through his hands. This scrupulous honesty astonished and delighted the British public. This man, who had only been known previously for his great eloquence in the House of Commons, had now proved himself to be of spotless honour with regard to money. The affection and confidence of the public were gained for him at once, and he succeeded in retaining this confidence during the whole of his parliamentary career.

On two occasions of his life fortune favoured Pitt in a remarkable way. The Duchess of Marlborough, who had been fascinated by his eloquence in the House of Commons, left him a large sum of money upon her death, and at a later period Sir William Pynsent presented him with a splendid estate in Somersetshire and a handsome fortune, which relieved him from all the troubles that had beset him owing to his scanty income.

In 1754 Henry Pelham died, and the Duke of Newcastle became Prime Minister. Many word-pictures of this minister have been written by men of his time, and they all describe him as a contemptible creature who made himself ridiculous by his foolish behaviour on all occasions, and who owed his position to his high title, to the king's favour, to his own greediness for power, and to the unscrupulous manner in which he bribed the members of Parliament to support him.

No sooner was he placed in power than disasters began to overtake the country. A war broke out between France and Great Britain, and several defeats were suffered by the British army, chiefly owing to the incapacity and bad management of the British Government. Pitt denounced the Duke of Newcastle in Parliament, and the British public loudly condemned the conduct of the war.

The popular discontent grew with every defeat which still followed the British forces, and the Duke of Newcastle's ministry was forced to resign. All eyes were now turned upon Pitt, who was the people's hero. A ludicrous picture has been drawn by writers of that period of the Duke of Newcastle coming to Pitt with unmanly tears, slobbering and fawning upon him, and entreating Pitt to join him in a new ministry. But Pitt, with a pride of which he afterwards repented, disdained his entreaties and refused to hold office with him. The king, in spite of his great dislike to Pitt, was now obliged to ask him to form a ministry. For five months Pitt was Prime Minister. The Duke of Newcastle's bribes, however, had gained the old nobleman more support in Parliament than Pitt possessed by his honesty and genius, so that in spite of his popularity in the country, Pitt's ministry was overthrown.

Pitt was ambitious for power, but he was eager for it in order that he might raise the sinking fortunes of his country, and inspire the nation with the spirit of patriotism which it seemed to have lost. Like all men of genius, he had great confidence in his own ability. "My lord," he said one day to the Duke of Devonshire, "I am sure that I can save this country, and that no one else can."

He now saw that he had made a great mistake in not joining hands with the Duke of Newcastle, who was supported by a powerful party in the country. In spite of Pitt's great popularity he was not strong enough to resist the party which honestly supported his rival, or which had been bought over by him. He now determined to join the man he had formerly denounced, and who was still eager to be supported by him for the sake of his popularity. But he determined also that he would hold no part in the system of bribery and corruption which the Duke of Newcastle considered necessary in the art of government. A new ministry was formed, in which Pitt selected for himself the office of Secretary for War, and he left all the vile business of bribery to the Duke of Newcastle, who was placed at the head of the Treasury.

PITT IN POWER.

Pitt now directed his great genius to the war which was waging between Great Britain and France. With burning eloquence he represented to the people that the national honour was at stake, and that they must be generous with their money if they did not wish their country to be ignominious among nations. His words fired the hearts of the people, and Parliament voted enormous sums of money for the requirements of the war. Pitt was at length free to carry out his vast schemes of conquest. Expeditions were planned against all parts of the world in which the French had power, and Pitt selected his generals and officers with such a discriminating eye for merit, and raised the army and navy to such a high state of proficiency, that in all parts of the world British arms were victorious. There is no space here, nor is it necessary in this short biography of Pitt, to give an account of the battles which were fought and won by British forces during this period of our history. It suffices to say that when Pitt was at the height of his power, the British Empire was increased by India and Canada, and that the United Kingdom was more powerful amongst nations than France or Spain had been in their most prosperous days. The name of Pitt, "the Great Commoner," as he was called, was surrounded with a glory which made him appear terrible in the eyes of his enemies and sublime in the eyes of his own nation.

DARK DAYS.

At length, however, the wheel of fortune turned, and a great disaster occurred to lessen the greatness of the British Empire. In 1760, George II. died, and his grandson became George III. The new king was a thorough Englishman at heart, but he desired more power than his grandfather, and determined to rule as well as to reign. He had a great dislike to ministers of any kind, unless they were favourites of his own who simply carried out his wishes. Pitt was therefore the special object of his dislike, and he endeavoured to turn him out of office. People were now getting tired of the war with France, but Pitt considered that peace ought not to be declared, because he knew that the French had allied themselves with Spain and that the peace would only be kept until the enemy had made full preparations for resuming the war. As he could not prevent the Government from coming to terms with the French, he resigned his office in the ministry.

Two favourites of the king were placed in power—Lord Bute, an incapable and unpopular Scotsman, became Prime Minister, while George Grenville was the leader of the House of Commons.

Pitt's words now came true, and the peace which had been proclaimed against his advice, was broken by a declaration of war from Spain. It was not long before the king's favourite, Lord Bute, showed himself to be quite unable to conduct the government of the country, and he was obliged to resign his office.

Once more Pitt joined the Government. He was now an old man, broken in health and disheartened at the state of public affairs. He had accepted the title of the Earl of Chatham, and for this reason he had lost a good deal of the people's affection, who had loved to regard him as "the Great Commoner," whom no one could bribe with money or high titles, and whose greatest desire was to serve his country in the House of Commons under the plain but honourable title of Mr. William Pitt.

In 1765, a Bill was introduced by George Grenville, and passed by Parliament, which was the beginning of a great national disaster. The new Act was known as the Stamp Act, and it compelled the American colonists to write all their legal documents upon stamped paper which they were obliged to buy from the English Government. Many people regarded this tax as quite fair in itself, for it was only right that the American colonists should contribute to the public expenses of the great Empire to which they belonged. But the Act was unjust, because it was passed without the consent of the colonists themselves, and therefore it broke one of the laws of Magna Charta, which says that the people cannot be taxed without their consent. The Americans were as indignant at this tax as John Hampden and his friends had been with the tax of ship money in the reign of Charles I.

Many of them refused to carry on any trade with England until the Act was withdrawn. William Pitt took up their cause, and although he was so ill and so racked with pain that he had to be carried to Parliament and propped up in the House of Lords, he struggled to show, with occasional bursts of his old eloquence, that the colonists were right to resist the tax, and he urged Parliament to repeal it. This time the danger was averted. Pitt's arguments prevailed, and the Act was repealed.

His health improved for a while, and the brave old statesman once more undertook the responsibility of the office of Prime Minister. Soon, however, his health failed him entirely, and he returned a bodily and mental wreck to his country estate.

A foolish and incapable man named Lord North succeeded him as Prime Minister, and one of the first acts of his ministry was to place a heavy tax upon tea, glass and paper imported from the American colonies. Once more the American people were roused to indignation, but this time the British Government, encouraged by the king himself, refused to listen to the arguments or the entreaties of the colonists. Neither side would yield, and at length the Americans, conscious of the justice of their cause, resolved to defend their rights by force. War was declared against Great Britain, and the deplorable result was witnessed of two English-speaking nations, connected by the closest ties of kindred, history, and interests, spilling each other's blood in deadly conflict. As all the world knows, the Americans, headed by George Washington, were completely victorious, and on the 4th of July, 1776, they passed the famous

Declaration of Independence, which severed them entirely from the British Empire to which they had once belonged.

William Pitt, old and feeble, his great mind often giving way under the torments of his gout, still struggled in his saner moments to induce the Government to withdraw before it became too late.

His last appearance in Parliament was to denounce the folly of the Government for their obstinacy in resolving to tax the American colonists without their consent.

He was supported to his seat in Parliament by his son William, who was soon to become as great a statesman as his father, and by his son-in-law Lord Mahon. He was very ill, and his brain was so excited that his physician had strongly urged him to remain at home. As he entered the House of Lords the Peers made way for him respectfully, and he bowed to them with great courtesy. The old nobleman leant feebly on his crutch. He wore a rich velvet coat, and his face, worn and haggard with disease, was almost concealed beneath a large wig, so that only his hawk-like nose could be seen. When he began his speech it was at once evident that his mind was wandering. His words could not be distinguished for some time until his voice grew stronger, and now and again a sentence was heard containing something which reminded the audience that the speaker was William Pitt, whose voice had once resounded through the house with a burning eloquence which had conquered all men's hearts. The Peers listened to his confused and rambling words in deep silence and with profound pity. It is said that " the stillness

was so deep that the dropping of a handkerchief would have been heard." At last the Earl
of Chatham clasped his hand to his breast, and,
swaying backwards, fell in an apoplectic fit. He was
carried to an adjoining chamber and lingered long
enough to be taken to his country house at Hayes.
Here, surrounded by his wife and family, to whom
he had been a faithful husband and a tender father,
the great and noble old statesman expired.

Many faults might be mentioned in the life-story
of William Pitt, many shortcomings might be described in a word-picture of his character; but with
these we have nothing to do in this sketch of his
career. Let us only remember that he acted always
with a profound desire to do the best for his country,
and that the greatness of the British Empire is
largely owing to his patriotic and mighty genius.

Q

X.

CAPTAIN COOK

AND

THE EXPLORATION OF AUSTRALASIA.

JAMES COOK, one of the greatest of English navigators, was the son of an agricultural labourer. He was born at the little village of Marton, in Yorkshire, on the 27th of October, 1728. When he was eight years old his parents removed to the neighbouring village of Great Ayton, and he attended the village school, where he obtained all the education which was then considered sufficient for a boy of his class, namely, reading, writing, and arithmetic. At the age of thirteen his parents apprenticed him to a shopkeeper who conducted business in the fishing village of Staithes, about fifteen miles from Great Ayton

In this little Yorkshire village James Cook served his master, Mr. Sanderson, who kept a shop with drapery on the one side and grocery on the other. The 'prentice's duties were to clean the shop out, to put up the shutters at night and to take them down in the morning, to fetch and carry, to serve behind the counter, and to kill the cockchafers, beetles, and earwigs which invaded the sugary and spicy realms of the grocery department. At night he slept under the counter, and in return for his services he had a small wage and his meals. These last did not lack in quantity, but they were not rich in quality. A hunk of bread, some fat bacon, and a pot of beer were the usual rations of James the 'prentice.

On Sunday, when he had the whole day to him-

CAPTAIN COOK.

(From the Portrait by Dance in Greenwich Hospital.)

self, and on week-days when an errand led his willing footsteps to the little harbour, he would listen eagerly to the fishermen's yarns as they smoked their pipes on the beach. At these times, forgetting all about Mr. Sanderson and his grocery, he would gaze out to sea and watch the sunlight shining on the sails of a fishing-smack so that it looked like a ship of gold, or sparkling on the crests of the waves as they rippled towards the shore. Gradually a great longing grew up in his heart to sail away from Mr. Sanderson's shop, with its blackbeetles and earwigs; to sail far, far away, across the broad ocean, to the lands which the fisherfolk talked of over their pipes. One day when Mr. Sanderson came down into his shop early in the morning, he found that the shutters had not been taken down and that his 'prentice's bed had not been slept in. James Cook had gone! Like Robinson Crusoe, the music of the sea had enchanted him, and he had run away to become a sailor.

Very little is known of these early years of James Cook. It is certain, however, that he became an able seaman in the service of Messrs. Walker, shipowners, of Whitby. For several years he traded between Newcastle and Norway, and during this period he obtained a thorough knowledge of practical seamanship. In 1755 we learn that he was the mate of a merchant vessel which was lying at that time in the Thames. To be the mate of a good ship would have been the height of ambition of many a lad born in Cook's station of life, and it must have been with many pangs that Cook was obliged to give up his position.

At this time Great Britain was preparing for a war with France, which everyone knew might break out at any moment. The Government officials of the Admiralty were straining every nerve to get His Majesty's ships ready for active service, and the officers were ordered to man their ships at once, with volunteers, if possible, but, if not, by means of the "press." In every port from Wapping to Whitby, His Majesty's press-gangs, consisting of a petty officer and about half-a-dozen Jack Tars, were busy persuading any stout-looking fellow they could find to go aboard one of His Majesty's men-of-war. If he objected, well, a pair of handcuffs on his wrists and three stout fellows on either side of him soon convinced him that objections were in vain. In this way the Royal Navy was often recruited, from the days of Admiral Blake to Lord Nelson.

It was not very pleasant to be a pressed man on board a man-of-war, for there was plenty of flogging for them if they grumbled, and not much chance of promotion. It was far better to volunteer with a good will than to be taken by force, and this was the opinion of James Cook. He gave up his berth as mate and stepped down to Wapping, where he entered as an able seaman on board the *Eagle*. He served under Captain, afterwards Sir Hugh, Palliser, a brave sailor who became famous as an Arctic explorer. Cook sailed with him to Canada and took a part in the capture of Louisburg, where Wolfe first earned the title of hero. Shortly afterwards he was appointed, by the recommendation of Captain Palliser, to be master of H.M.S. *Mercury*, and during the siege of Quebec he distinguished himself by taking soundings of the River St. Lawrence and making a chart for the guidance of the fleet, under the most difficult and dangerous circumstances.

It is a remarkable thing that a man who entered the navy "before the mast," that is to say, as a common seaman, should have attained the rank of master in so short a time, or, indeed, in any time. The master of a vessel was responsible for the sailing of the ship. That a common seaman, with all the disadvantages of a lack of education and with his time considerably occupied by his duties, should have obtained the highly scientific knowledge necessary for the navigation of a vessel, the writing of a ship's log, and the making of a chart, is extraordinary, and very much to Cook's honour.

COOK'S FIRST VOYAGE TO THE PACIFIC.

In 1768 Cook was given the command of an enterprise which was to bring him a world-wide fame and to add his name to the honourable roll of the world's greatest explorers. In this year, the Royal Society, which was, and still is, a society of the most learned scientific men of this country, drew up a memorial to the king, informing him that an important astronomical event would take place in June, and as it could best be observed from some place in the Pacific Ocean, they proposed that an expedition should be sent out by the Government to make observations, and at the same time to bring to light some of the secrets of the Pacific.

King George was pleased with the idea, and commanded a vessel to be equipped and sent out in command of any scientific naval officer recommended by the Royal Society. It speaks well for Cook's reputation and learning that he should have been the man picked out amongst all others to conduct the expedition. But so it was. He was raised to the rank of lieutenant and placed in command of a stout vessel designed by himself, and built by his old masters, the Walkers, of Whitby. On the 26th of

August, 1768, the good ship *Endeavour*, as she was
called, sailed from Deptford to Plymouth, and from
the port out of which Drake had sailed so often to
earn an undying fame, this new voyage of discovery

THE *ENDEAVOUR* APPROACHING TAHITI.

set sail. The crew consisted of eighty-five men,
including the captain, and they took with them
a few distinguished men of science.

The *Endeavour* touched at Madeira, then at Rio
de Janeiro in South America, and at last rounded
Cape Horn and entered the South Pacific Ocean in
January of the following year. For four months the

vessel ploughed that mighty ocean whose secrets were guarded so jealously from prying eyes. On his way to Tahiti, Cook discovered many islands which had been quite unknown before, and marked them down on the charts which he was preparing for the use of future navigators. On April 13th they arrived at Tahiti, where they spent three months enjoying the beauty of the island, and enquiring into the manners and language of the natives, who received them in a very friendly manner. The astronomical observations were successfully taken, and at last, with great reluctance on the part of the crew, they set sail once more and directed their course into the unknown seas.

After a voyage of six weeks, during which they never once saw land, they sighted the pine-clad hills and the dim outline of the mountain ranges of North Island, New Zealand. When they first attempted to land, the natives attacked them with great bravery, and they were obliged to retreat to the ship. They became more friendly, however, when they saw that the strangers were peacefully inclined, but their friendship was not much more agreeable than their ill will, for they stole everything they could lay their hands upon.

Cook sailed along the coast, fighting or trading with the natives according to the manner in which they received him. At last, after sailing completely round North Island, he anchored in Queen Charlotte's Sound on the north coast of South Island. Here he landed and hoisted the Union Jack, taking possession of the country in the name of King George III.

At the end of nineteen days the *Endeavour* came within sight of a long coast line. Captain Cook, standing on the quarter deck of his stout little vessel, shading the sun from his eyes as he gazed towards the land, saw for the first time the great island of Australia.

As they approached the coast they found that the cliffs formed a steep wall which barred their landing. At last they anchored in Botany Bay, which was given the name by Cook, on account of the numerous plants of a previously unknown character which were gathered by the scientific men of the party. From this bay they sailed round the coast, anchoring now and again in other bays and trying to establish a friendship with the natives.

At first the inhabitants of the country showed a very warlike behaviour, and hurled spears at the Englishmen, until a few musket shots sent them flying in a terrible panic. By degrees Cook and his men succeeded in coming to friendly terms with them; but, like the New Zealanders, they were dreadful thieves. Later on, indeed, their behaviour became still more unpleasant, for they set fire to the dry grass near Cook's encampment, and the flames spread with the rapidity of the "bush fires" which have been such a source of danger to the British colonists who have since made their homes in the country which Cook was the first to explore. The fire destroyed Cook's camp, and he had to put out to sea again sooner than he intended.

Once more the *Endeavour* made its way along the coast, sailing in a northerly direction and rounding Cape York. Cook now landed on a little island near this cape and, hoisting the Union Jack, amid the

cheers of his crew, he gave the name of New South
Wales to the whole of the eastern coast of Australia
which he had explored, and he took possession of it
in the name of King George.

Now, after so many valuable discoveries, he resolved
to set out on the homeward journey. Accordingly he
sailed to New Guinea, thence to the Cape of Good
Hope, and so home.

By this voyage the great navigator let a flood of
light upon the vast country of Australia, upon the
great islands of New Zealand, and upon a cluster of
smaller islands which had until then been hidden in
the untracked waves of the Pacific Ocean.

But the expedition, which was to add thousands
of square miles to the British Empire, was not
accomplished without enormous difficulties and hard-
ships. Only a man of Cook's unflagging determination and of his unflinching courage could have held
on his course in spite of the disease, the lack of food,
the discontent of the crew, and the dangers from
storms, from shipwrecks, and from natives, which he
had to encounter. Out of the eighty-five men who
had sailed with him from Plymouth Sound, only
fifty-five returned home with him. No less than
thirty had fallen victims to that fearful sailors'
disease, the scurvy.

Who can describe the horrors of a voyage in a
tropical climate, where no land is seen week after week,
while the hot sun pours fiercely down upon the salt
water, dazzling the eyes of the sailors; when the
victuals fall short, and only salt meat and rotten,
maggoty biscuits are left to appease the gnawing
pangs of hunger; when every day a sailor is added to

the sick list, while red blotches appear all over his skin and his gums begin to bleed, so that the doctor shakes his head mournfully and mutters "Scurvy!" when every now and again the captain reads the burial service over some poor lad whose body is cast overboard, while the sailors stare gloomily and ask "Who will be the next?" when the captain sits in his cabin studying his chart, or stands on deck straining his eyes for land, and wonders how long it will be before his half-starved, scurvy-stricken, woebegone crew break out into open mutiny? He who can imagine all this can realise the sufferings of Cook and his sailors.

For hardly one year after this long voyage was Cook allowed to live in peace and quiet, and before the year was out he was busily preparing for another enterprise.

"THE GREAT SOUTHERN CONTINENT."

At that time a great number of scientific men declared that a vast continent existed which stretched for thousands of miles from the Pacific Ocean to the South Pole. Innumerable legends had grown up about this Great Southern Continent, as it was called. Many people believed that it was inhabited by a highly civilised race of white people, that it contained towns more splendid than the richest cities of the Indian Empire, and that more wealth might be found in this wonderful country than in all the gold mines of the Indies. Several Dutch navigators who had sailed into the Pacific Ocean before Captain Cook himself, had descried islands in the South Seas which they had imagined to be part of the Great Southern

Continent, and their reports had encouraged the general belief in this imaginary country.

Cook himself half believed that such a continent might exist, and when the Government invited him to make a new voyage of discovery in order to decide this question he readily undertook the new and dangerous enterprise.

Two vessels, built for endurance rather than for speed, and called the *Resolution* and the *Adventure*, were fitted up with every requirement for a long voyage. Captain Cook sailed on board the *Resolution* with one hundred and twelve men, and Captain Tobias Furneaux commanded the *Adventure* with eighty-one men.

The ships sailed from Plymouth Sound on the 13th day of July, 1772. They made their way to the Cape of Good Hope, and then, steering a southerly course, they met the floating icebergs of the South Pacific Ocean. For six weeks they sailed among the icebergs, getting farther and farther south. Two or three men were attacked with scurvy, but Captain Cook had learnt a painful lesson from his last voyage, and he had now come provided with a quantity of sour-kraut, lemon juice, marmalade and the juice of wort. Every day he dosed the crew with these medicines, in spite of their grumbling, and he was always careful that the men should have plenty of exercise and salt bathing. By these wise precautions he succeeded in saving his crew from the dreadful plague of scurvy, and during the whole voyage not one man fell a victim to this disease. This was a great victory in the story of the sea. Every year hundreds of sailors had succumbed to the scurvy, and Cook was the first to prove that by careful diet and proper precautions it might be averted.

After a weary voyage among the icebergs the *Resolution* at last encountered a long and impenetrable field of ice, so that it was quite impossible to proceed further south. Captain Cook had now proved beyond a doubt that the Great Southern Continent existed only in imagination, and that a vast realm of unbroken ice extended throughout the Antarctic Circle.

The *Resolution* had become separated from her comrade, the *Adventure*, but they rejoined one another in Dusky Sound, New Zealand, to which Cook directed his ship. After having completely circumnavigated the Globe in or near the Antarctic Circle, and having sailed more than thrice that distance in their numerous explorations, the English seamen reached their native shore on July 30th, 1775, after an absence of three years and sixteen days.

THE LAST VOYAGE.

Captain Cook's last voyage was to discover that famous North-West Passage from the Atlantic to the Pacific, which has been the ambition and the death of so many explorers. Unlike his predecessors, Cook endeavoured to enter the passage from the Pacific instead of from the Atlantic. He took a roundabout course and touched at New Zealand, and thence proceeded to the island of Hawaii.

Here, in one of the loveliest spots of the earth, the great navigator met his death. The natives of this island received him at first with an enthusiasm

and respect amounting almost to worship.   This
friendliness lasted until the English seamen took
their departure.   Unfortunately an accident occurred
which obliged Captain Cook to return to the island
in order to repair the damage.   For some unknown
reason the behaviour of the natives suddenly changed.
They were insolent and unfriendly, and after several
small thefts they stole one of the *Resolution's* boats.
This was more than Captain Cook could allow to
go unpunished.   He put off from the *Resolution*
with three boats, in which were nearly forty sailors
armed with muskets and cutlasses.   He then proceeded to the chief's house, accompanied by a few
of the sailors, and he was about to demand that
his boat should be restored, when a native came
running up with the news that the Englishmen in
one of the boats had fired upon a native and killed
him.   At this news the natives were very much
enraged.   They pressed round Captain Cook with
threatening looks and cries, and many of them ran
for their spears and clubs.   At last they handled
him so roughly that Captain Cook tried to beat them
back with the butt end of his musket.   Fearing
that matters were now becoming very serious, Cook
ordered the sailors to retreat, and he was about to
follow them when he saw with dismay that the
sailors in the boats, alarmed for his safety, had
begun to fire among the natives, thus enraging
them to a greater fury.   He waved his hand
and tried to order his men to cease firing, but
they could not hear his voice above the yells of
the natives.   Suddenly one of the chiefs, more
daring than his comrades, darted behind the captain

and stabbed him in the back with a dagger. Then a number of the natives dashed upon him, and, after holding him under the water for a while, beat him upon the rocks until his body was mangled beyond recognition. The other sailors were fiercely attacked, and after three of them had been killed, the rest managed to escape in the boats.

Such was the tragic end of one of the greatest navigators of the world.

In this short account of Cook's life it has only been possible to give the barest outline of his great achievements, but all the details of his voyages, all the adventures he encountered, the wonderful and beautiful places he discovered, the customs and behaviour of the natives, and a host of entertaining facts are described in the narrative of his voyages, which he himself wrote, and which may now be read in many inexpensive books.

Captain Cook was not the first European to behold the coasts of Australia and New Zealand, for some early Dutch navigators had touched these shores, but he was the first to obtain any accurate knowledge of these beautiful lands. He made a clear track across the Pacific Ocean dotted with the islands which he had discovered, so that his countrymen were able to follow in his wake to make their fortunes or their homes in those flowery lands of the southern seas, which are now among the most prosperous colonies of the British Empire.

XI.

NELSON AND WELLINGTON

THE DEFENCE OF THE EMPIRE.

IN 1793 the French people, who had been ground
down for centuries by the nobility of their country,
rose against their oppressors, and that terrible revo-
lution took place which bathed France in the blood
of its nobles, and to which King Louis XVI. and
his beautiful wife, Marie Antoinette, fell victims.
The people gained a terrible victory, and the French
Republic was established. "Liberty, Equality, and
Fraternity" were the watchwords of the Republicans,
but in the height of their triumph this noble ideal
was quite forgotten, and the streets of Paris ran red
with the blood of those considered to be enemies
of the Republic by the people's leaders, who were
bloodthirsty and brutal tyrants a hundred times
worse than the nobles.

At last the people grew weary of bloodshed and
of the continual revolutions among the leaders
themselves, and they looked for a man strong
enough to establish order in their distracted
country. One was found in a young general named
Napoleon Buonaparte. He had distinguished himself

by defeating the Austrians, who had declared war against the French Republic. Then he carried the war into Italy, and victory after victory followed his soldiers. The French people now became mad for military glory, and Napoleon Buonaparte was made

NAPOLEON BUONAPARTE.

the head of the French Republic and, afterwards, the first Emperor of France.

Napoleon was one of the greatest and one of the most unscrupulous generals the world has ever seen. European nations trembled before the genius and the huge ambition of this man who wished to make

P

every civilised country a province of the French Empire Austria, Italy, Spain, Denmark, and Russia were conquered, or submitted to the supremacy of Napoleon.

Only one country was powerful enough to resist this universal conqueror. In 1793 the French Republic declared war against Great Britain, and for twenty-two years, with only one short intermission, a deadly struggle took place between the two nations. During that period England was many times in terrible danger, but at last, owing to the courage and genius of our soldiers and sailors, Napoleon was overthrown and peace was restored to Europe.

In that time of danger so many of our countrymen proved themselves to be heroes on land and sea that to describe their gallant deeds would take many more pages than this little volume contains. The names of those splendid sea-heroes, Nelson, Howe, Jervis, Duncan, Collingwood, Hardy, and Riou, should ring with a familiar and glorious sound in the ears of every British citizen, while no less splendid are the names of Wellington, Moore, and Napier, who led British armies to the victories which gave peace and safety to our country and to Europe.

Among all the gallant sailors of that time the name of Horatio Nelson stands foremost and shines brightest. It was to his genius that the safety of this country was due when terrible disaster might have been its fate if a man less skilful had been in command of the British fleet. The battle of Trafalgar, in which Nelson gave up his life for his country, saved England from the foreign invasion which had threatened it, and gained for our country the supremacy of the seas which we have kept from that day to this.

Horatio Nelson was born, in 1758, at the little village of Burnham Thorpe, in Norfolk, where his father was rector. He entered the navy at twelve years of age, and, in spite of being very delicate, he obtained rapid promotion owing to the influence of his uncle, Captain Suckling, and his own ability. His early years were spent in voyages to the Arctic regions, to the East and West Indies, and to Canada. When war broke out with the French Republic he was appointed captain of the *Agamemnon*, and ordered to the Mediterranean to attack Corsica. At the sieges of Bastia and Calvi he played a distinguished part, but during the attack on Calvi he was unfortunate enough to lose the sight of his right eye, which was injured by some gravel cast up by a shot. This accident did not daunt his ardent spirit, and shortly afterwards he rendered splendid service to his country in several engagements with the enemy.

THE VICTORY OFF CAPE ST. VINCENT.

It was at the battle of Cape St. Vincent that Nelson first proved himself to be one of the most daring and brilliant naval commanders. In February, 1797, Nelson, on board the *Captain*, joined the fleet under Admiral Sir John Jervis, which was sailing off the south-west coast of Spain on the look out for the Spanish fleet, which was then on the side of the French. The enemy was sighted on February

15th, 1797, outnumbering the English by twelve battleships and six frigates. Sir John Jervis gave the signal to attack at once. The brunt of the battle fell upon Nelson's ship, the *Captain*, which he had to defend for a time against the combined forces of seven Spanish battleships. When the *Captain* was so crippled that not a sail or rope was left, Nelson ordered his men to grapple her alongside the *San Nicolas*. Then he jumped into the Spanish battleship, followed by his men, and going from deck to deck, they beat back the Spanish officers and sailors and took possession of the ship. A volley of musketry now met them from another Spanish battleship, which lay alongside the *San Nicolas*. With superb audacity Nelson gave orders for his men to board the second vessel from the decks of the *San Nicolas*. With a shout of " Westminster Abbey or victory ! " meaning that he would die gloriously or conquer, he led the way himself into the *San Josef*. The Spanish officers soon surrendered, and the famous scene took place when Nelson stood on the quarter-deck of the *San Josef* and received the officers' swords one by one as a token of their surrender, and handed them on to an old sailor named William Fearney, who tucked them under his arm with perfect coolness. For his splendid services in this battle Nelson was made a Knight of the Bath, and became a rear-admiral of the British fleet.

During an attack upon Santa Cruz, which proved unsuccessful, Nelson had the misfortune to lose his right arm. This accident disabled him for a time, and he was obliged to return to

England, where he lay for several months in great agony, but as soon as he could he struggled on board ship again, for he was eager to return to active service.

THE BATTLES OF THE NILE AND COPENHAGEN.

In 1798 Napoleon set sail for Egypt with a French army. His great ambition was not content with having brought the greater part of Europe under his dominion, but he now hoped to found an empire in the east. Nelson was ordered to attack his fleet when and where he could find it. Unfortunately he could obtain no information as to its whereabouts until Napoleon's army had landed in Egypt, and t` French battleships were lying at anchor in the Bay of Aboukir, near one of the mouths of the river Nile. Here Nelson discovered them at last. The French admiral had drawn up his ships close to the shore, and thought that no British battleship would dare to pass inside his line for fear of grounding. But Nelson dared everything. Boldly he led his ship inside the French line, and although one of them, the *Culloden*, ran aground, the others passed safely and poured their broadsides into the French fleet. All through the night the battle raged, and in the morning thirteen out of the seventeen French battleships were captured, burnt, or sunk.

Nelson's next great battle was at Copenhagen, where he had been directed to destroy the Danish navy, which Napoleon had forced to side with him. The Danish fleet consisted of fifty-one vessels, and the shore bristled with batteries, while the entrance to the harbour was exceedingly difficult to navigate owing to shoals. Every preparation had been made for a vigorous defence, and the Danish sailors, who, next to the English, were the best and bravest in the world, were determined to defend their vessels to the last gasp. Such was the enemy which Nelson was directed to attack with only twelve ships of the line and a number of frigates.

The British fleet was under the supreme command of Admiral Sir Hyde Parker, but he gave Nelson a free hand in the conduct of the battle until he should direct otherwise. Nelson began the attack with his usual boldness, but he was unfortunate enough to lose the service of a fourth of his fleet, which ran aground, or was otherwise prevented by the currents and shoals from coming into action. With the remnants of his fleet Nelson attacked the Danes, and was received with the fire of a thousand guns. A terrible battle followed, in which the English chances seemed so desperate that Admiral Parker signalled to Nelson to retreat. But Nelson was a man to whom death was sweeter than retreat, and with bitter humour he put his telescope to his blind eye and exclaimed, " I really do not see the signal. Keep mine for closer battle flying! That's the way I answer such signals. Nail mine to the mast!" So the battle went on, and ill it was for the Danes that it did so. The little British fleet under Nelson fought with such fierce energy that, in spite of the great bravery of the Danes, Nelson gained a great and complete victory.

NELSON COMING ON DECK BEFORE THE BATTLE OF TRAFALGAR.

"'TWAS IN TRAFALGAR'S BAY."

And now only one other victory remained for
Nelson to gain before he finished his life's work.
Who does not know the story of Trafalgar, in which
Nelson died in the hour of triumph?

Buonaparte was determined to destroy the power
of the only nation he feared, and he assembled
a great army at Boulogne for the invasion of England. But before a French army could set foot on
English soil they would have to cross that "silver
streak" which lies between England and France,
and to prevent this was the work of Nelson and
his comrades.

For many weary months Nelson watched the
French fleet lying in Toulon, waiting its opportunity
to slip out so that it could join another fleet at
Brest, and then conduct the army of Boulogne to the
English shore. This plan nearly succeeded. The
fleet at Toulon slipped past Nelson, and although
he chased it as far as the West Indies he did not
succeed in catching it. Then he returned with all
speed, despairing at the thought that the invasion
might have taken place during his absence. Luckily,
however, this was not so; and on the 21st of October,
1805, Nelson, in command of twenty-seven battleships, fell in with the combined French and Spanish
fleets, consisting of thirty-three ships, under Admirals
Villeneuve and Gravina, off Cape Trafalgar in the
south-west of Spain.

Nelson held a council of war with his officers on
board his flagship, the *Victory*, and, having given
them his plan of battle, he gave that famous
signal to the fleet which has been the watchword of

Englishmen ever since : " England expects every man will do his duty." The signal was received with cheer upon cheer from every sailor in the fleet, and then the battle began. The result of that battle is

NELSON'S DEATH IN THE COCKPIT OF THE *VICTORY*.
(From the Picture by F. W. Devis.)

known to all the world. The French and Spanish ships were nearly all captured or destroyed, and Nelson gained a victory which saved this country from all fear of invasion and utterly destroyed Napoleon's power on the seas.

But in the hour of that splendid victory the brave admiral was struck down by a bullet fired from the tops of the French ship *Redoubtable.* He was carried down to the cock-pit mortally wounded, and died three hours after. The last words which left his lips were, "Thank God, I have done my duty."

THE IRON DUKE.

The French power at sea had been shattered, but everywhere on land the French armies were still victorious. England now had need of a soldier who could check this triumphal march of conquest. For several years it had seemed as if British generals and British soldiers had lost their skill and daring, but at last a man was found with genius enough to defeat the generals of the Emperor Napoleon, who had never known defeat before. This was Arthur Wellesley, afterwards Duke of Wellington.

Wellesley had first won renown in India, when, in 1803, he won the battle of Assaye, in which 4,500 troops under his command utterly defeated an army of 30,000 men under a rebellious native prince. He was recalled from India shortly after this victory to command a small force of British troops in Portugal. At this time Spain had submitted to Napoleon, who had placed his brother Joseph on the throne; but Portugal still held out against the French, and refused to obey Napoleon's orders to close its harbours to British ships. Napoleon's generals advanced into Portugal to bring the country to subjection, and when Sir Arthur Wellesley set foot on Portuguese soil he found that Lisbon was already captured. But now, to the astonishment of the whole world, the French army, composed of veterans who had been victorious in every battle but this, were utterly defeated at Vimeira by the British force of young and inexperienced soldiers under Wellesley

This victory, which drove the French from Portugal, and which was the first in the famous Peninsular War, was followed by a series of splendid victories in Spain, which Wellesley, or Viscount Wellington, as he now became, gained over the veteran troops and the most distinguished soldiers of France. Talavera, Albuera, Badajoz, Salamanca, and Vittoria are the names of those battles, in which no general ever displayed a greater genius for war than Wellington, and in which no British troops ever played a more glorious part than the young soldiers who became heroes under Wellington's stern training and discipline.

Never once did Wellington suffer a defeat, although many a time he was in danger of being annihilated by the superior forces of the French. But what is still more to his honour is that he taught his soldiers the great lesson of humanity in war. The French armies had often disgraced their victories by plundering and ravaging the country through which they marched, but Wellington sternly enforced upon his soldiers his absolute commands to refrain from these horrible usages of warfare. Constantly he urged his officers and men to treat the inhabitants of the country with courtesy and consideration, and if any of the troops transgressed these demands Wellington punished them with a severity which made them tremble.

Towards the end of the Peninsular War the great
tyrant of Europe, Napoleon Buonaparte, was thrown
from the height of his power. Encouraged by the
British successes, the other nations of Europe had
regained spirit and rose against their taskmaster.
Russia, Prussia and Austria, Portugal and Spain.

THE DUKE OF WELLINGTON.

(From the Picture by Sir William Beecher, R..A.)

combined with Great Britain against their common
enemy. At last, on the 16th of October, 1813,
Napoleon was utterly defeated at the great battle of
Leipsic. Six months later he found himself without
resources, and was forced to resign his throne. He
was sent to the island of Elba, and at length, **in**
1814, Europe found peace.

This peace did not last long. In the month of March, 1815, Napoleon escaped from his island prison and landed at Cannes in the south of France. In a short time a great French army gathered round him, ready to confront the whole world under the great Emperor who had led them so often to victory.

THE BATTLE OF WATERLOO.

On the 18th of June, 1815, at Waterloo, near Brussels, the great battle took place in which the Emperor Napoleon made one last great and desperate effort to regain his power, and in which a British army under the Duke of Wellington, aided later in the day by a Prussian army under Marshal Blücher, fought for the liberty and peace of Europe.

Wellington was in command of 67,600 men, of whom more than half were Belgians, Dutch, and other foreigners. The French army amounted to 71,900 men.

On the morning of Sunday, the 18th of June, the battle began. Wellington issued his commands as if he were on a drill ground, and this calm courage of the "Iron Duke," as he was called, inspired perfect confidence in his officers and men. Many books have been written describing "king-making Waterloo," but here there is only space for a few words.

Many Belgian troops fled from the field at the beginning of the battle, but the British regiments, in spite of containing a large number of young soldiers who had never smelt powder before, behaved with the most splendid bravery. Every officer acted as if the whole battle depended upon him alone, every soldier fought regardless of danger and with a hero's courage.

No less brave were the French troops. They attacked the British army again and again with fierce ardour, only to be beaten back by the volleys of the British musketry, the fire of the British cannon. Time after time the French cavalry, who had won glory in a hundred fights, charged with fury upon the British squares, but again and again they were shattered against the impenetrable ranks of the British infantry. At length, Napoleon, with a last desperate effort, ordered a final attack to be made by the whole of his Old Guard, the flower of his army. With glorious and pathetic courage these brave veterans tried to turn the tide of battle, but they too were at last shattered and driven back in hopeless retreat. Then Wellington, seeing that the moment of victory was at hand, ordered an advance of the whole army. The British cavalry swept down upon the disordered masses of the retreating French army, while the British infantry drove them back at the bayonet point. At this point Marshal Blücher came upon the scene with his Prussians, and turned the French retreat into an utter and overwhelming defeat. Napoleon himself escaped, but was afterwards captured and imprisoned in the island of St. Helena, where he ended his wonderful career. Peace was restored to Europe, never to be disturbed again by this ambitious soldier, and England has never since been in danger of a foreign invasion.

The Duke of Wellington had done his great work as a general, and the rest of his life was spent in the peaceful, but not less honourable, work of a statesman. Although he was the greatest general England has ever possessed, he always spoke earnestly in favour of peace, and when anyone reminded him of his own military glory he always answered that

THE WELLINGTON MEMORIAL IN ST. PAUL'S CATHEDRAL

even in the hour of victory he had never been able to forget the awful horrors and tragedies of war.

In 1852 the "Iron Duke" died, after a long life spent in the service of his country, and was buried in St. Paul's Cathedral, "to the noise of the mourning of a mighty nation."

Such were some of the men who helped in the foundation of the British Empire, which to-day holds such a great and honourable position among nations. Many faults they may have had, but they were men with a mighty courage, whose hearts burned with a noble desire to serve their country honourably and faithfully, and who were eager to devote their whole lives, and if need be to die, in order that they might help to make the British Empire powerful, prosperous, and glorious.

PRINTED BY CASSELL & COMPANY, LIMITED, LA BELLE SAUVAGE, LONDON, E.C.

20.907

Lightning Source UK Ltd.
Milton Keynes UK
UKHW020407081118
331957UK00009B/697/P

9 780483 304697